Herbs and the Earth

Herbs and the Earth

By HENRY BESTON

Introduction by ROGER B. SWAIN

Woodcuts by JOHN HOWARD BENSON

DAVID R. GODINE, PUBLISHER, BOSTON

HOUSTON PUBLIC LIBRARY

This edition published in 1990 by
David R. Godine, Publisher, Inc.
Horticultural Hall
300 Massachusetts Avenue
Boston, Massachusetts 02115

Library of Congress Cataloging-in-Publication Data
Beston, Henry, 1888-1968.
Herbs and the earth / Henry Beston; woodcuts by John Howard
Benson.—New ed.
p.   cm.
ISBN 0-87923-827-5
1. Herbs. 2. Herb gardening. 3. Herbs—Folklore.
4. Nature. I. Title.
SB351.H5B4   1990   89-46185
581.6'3—dc20   CIP

First offset printing, 1990

Printed in the United States of America

To
Two Young Persons
Who Never Pull up or Step on
Father's Herbs

Contents

Illustrations

Introduction

Five chimneys anchor the roofline of the next-to-last farmhouse on East-Neck Road in Nobleboro, Maine. They replace a single massive central chimney, built with the house in 1814, but dismantled sometime at the turn of the century in favor of multiple chimneys and individual wood stoves. New England architecture is like this. Each new generation leaves its marks—an added shed, a dormer, a porch, a barn razed or raised. The accumulated layers of clapboard and shingle, wallpaper and paint, chronicle human settlement here as surely as the stonewalls that lead into the woods.

Henry Beston's long tenure at Chimney Farm began almost by accident. On a Maine visit to his friend Jake Day he went to look at a place for sale on "the Neck," as the locals refer to the peninsula that divides Damariscotta Lake. This was early in 1931, and nearly five feet of snow lay on the ground. Beston, who was something of an iconoclast in matters of dress, cut quite a figure wearing his Piccadilly blue overcoat and a pair of borrowed snowshoes as he hiked across the buried pasture and down through the old-growth hemlock and pines to the edge of the snow-covered ice.

Later, back home in Hingham, Massachusetts, he would ask his wife Elizabeth Coatsworth—the poet and children's author—whether she would like to have a Maine farm, but he already had his answer. The hundred acres, with its woodlot partially enclosing Deep Cove, would be a sanctuary from "the modern city with its violences and barbarities." And so it was until his death in 1968, and hers in 1986. Though the two of them would travel elsewhere—to Arizona, the Yucatan, and especially the French parts of Canada— Maine was to be Henry Beston's chosen state, his chosen home. Today a massive boulder, shaded by sugar maple trees, marks the couple's grave in the little burial plot just across the road.

By birth, Beston's allegiances lay still farther east. Christened Henry Beston Sheahan, he was the son of an Irish physician father and a French-Catholic mother. Born in Quincy, Massachusetts, in 1888, he was raised bilingually and would later claim that he could think as freely in French as in English. He attended Harvard College, majored in English, and stayed in Cambridge for a master's degree before going abroad to teach at the University of Lyons. There, in the vineyards and villages of southern France, he seems to have been particularly struck by the centuries of unbroken agricultural tradition. The experience would echo years later in Maine when he wrote his wife from Chimney Farm: "I heard across the lovely, wet, sunlit, autumn countryside the rumble of a farm-cart's wheel and the fine challenge of a cock, and hearing them I thought of how all these earthy things carry me back to France, back to Ste. Catherine-sous-Rivière . . . the first place in which I encountered and knew and loved the earth."

Many years intervened, however, including the First World War with its "parachute trench lights fizzing magnesium-white over trees" and the "drifting miles of wreckage" at sea. Beston drove an ambulance and later served as a Navy correspondent in the submarine zones. His first book—*A Volunteer Poilu* (1916)—chronicled his war experiences and was published under the name of Sheahan, but shortly thereafter the author began living and writing as Henry Beston, using the surname of his maternal grandmother's family. The next decade found him back in Boston working in the *Atlantic Monthly* editorial offices, and on a string of books for children. These he said he wrote mostly to get the war out of his mind.

By 1926, he was still single and had recently had a small cottage built on a fifty-acre parcel of barrier beach he owned in the town of Eastham on Cape Cod. What began as a two-week visit there turned into a year-long stay in the dunes, with his nearest neighbor the Nauset coast guard station two miles north up the beach. From his journals of that year containing his accounts of life at the edge of the surf, the pageant of birds, storms, and constellations, he wrote *The Outermost House* (1928). By far the most famous of Beston's books, this landmark of natural-history writing put The Fo'castle —the name Beston gave to his two-room cottage— into literary gazetteers right alongside Thoreau's cabin in Concord. But Beston never encouraged the comparison, saying that "Thoreau had very little heart." And it must be noted that Beston's own heart belonged more to Maine than Massachusetts.

Once the family owned Chimney Farm, he rarely returned to Cape Cod.

The Bestons' move to Maine was a gradual one. In 1931, Elizabeth was expecting the couple's second child, and so Henry was left to supervise the next round of renovations at Chimney Farm alone: plumbing to replace the pump in the kitchen, a bathroom, and an open porch between the dining room and the kitchen ell. He also returned the original twelve-pane sashes to the windows, and repainted the fading yellow exterior a farmhouse red.

Construction completed, the family began spending every summer in Maine. They made up for the natural shortness of the season by coming early and staying late, even when it meant taking the two girls north a few weeks before school ended each year, and missing the start of school in the fall. During the off-season, they returned to Maine for a week whenever they could, switching in Portland from the Boston and Maine to the Maine Central Railroad for the ride to the flag-stop in Nobleboro. A dozen years later, in 1944, the Bestons moved north for good.

Until then Henry chafed at having to live and write in suburbia during part of the year. "There is no nature for a naturalist to see, there are no birds save The Spotted Chevrolet and the Greater and Lesser Buick," he complained to a family friend. "Boston Harbor, which lies in front of the house and beyond the cars, has absolutely no meaning to me in terms of beauty and the spirit; it is nothing but a glacial spillover surrounding a *tub de mud*."

At Chimney Farm, by contrast, Henry lived by agricultural time. Seasons here were distinguished less by the position of Orion than by oxen ploughing in the spring, the flash of scythes in summer, apple harvesting, a dish of Indian pudding with light cream on a mid-winter night. The Bestons made no great effort to run their place as a farm. Not until after Henry's death did Elizabeth and her younger daughter Catherine begin raising draft horses. But the neighbors looked benevolently on these outsiders. Henry seems to have had that grace of personality—missing in many who embrace the solitude of writing—that made him comfortable and welcome in many settings. On his own land or on others', he sought the company of rural people. In their husbandry he found the "poignant and poetic recognition of the long continuity of man" that was his own real calling.

For *Herbs and the Earth* (1935), there was first the herb garden. On the side of the house facing the lake lay The Court, so-called because it was bounded on two sides by the main house and the kitchen ell, and on a third by a copse of chokecherries. Here Beston began with a ten-foot bed of herbs, that expanded with his experience and enthusiasm into a pair of beds. One of these faced east toward the water, and contained the moisture-needing mints. The other lay perpendicular, facing south, for the sun-loving species like lavender and thyme. Though he corresponded widely with other herbalists, and spent time in their gardens, Beston deliberately kept his own herb garden small, the better to understand the plants he was raising.

"Part garden book, part musing study of our relation to Nature through the oldest group of plants known to gardeners," was how Beston described the following chapters. The gardening part is sound—for instance, his advice to group the Mediterranean herbs and to mulch more during hot weather. But herbs are a forgiving class of plants. They do not need particularly rich soils, and their own natural fragrance is their self-defense against insects. "Creative work with the soil and the contemplation of nature" might "make the two best pillars of our lives as human beings," but Beston was better at one than the other. According to Elizabeth, "Henry, dressed in his oldest working clothes, would go out to sit beside the border staring down at it. At long intervals he might crumble a piece of earth between his fingers, or pull up a weed. But mostly he was just staring and staring. When he came in, he would say, 'I've been working in the herb garden all morning.'"

Much of the actual physical work in the herb garden, as elsewhere at Chimney Farm, was done by one of the ten sons from a neighboring family. Beston's labor was chiefly to refine the essence of insight from the bulk of herbiage. From the plainest leaf, he could take the "pulse of the year." To him even the smallest collection contained something "of earth and of time and of magic and of peace." There is basil, "predetermined to symmetry," sage, with its "pebbled leaves silvered over with a summer dew," "the divine mind itself reflected" in the blue blossoms of borage.

With a handful of exceptions—bayberry, bee balm, wintergreen—our garden herbs are all Eurasian immigrants. Tracing their history allowed Beston to return again to his own roots. He could not speak of them without invoking the Bible, Greeks, Romans, Charlemagne, the Middle Ages, the Renaissance, and Elizabethan England. Studying his herbs, he pored through French catalogs, deciphering the fragrances of his youth. In culture and emotion, as much as by the compass, the herb gardens at Chimney Farm faced east.

As he was composing *Herbs and the Earth*, Henry Beston's class at Harvard celebrated its 25th reunion. From the quiet of birches at the edge of his field, he offered up his own recipe for the future: "The earth has its own peace," Beston wrote his classmates; "to be in religious and poetic relation to the mystery of earth and sky and the living thing, to know that life is a stream, a flowing . . . is a light safe from time and any storm." He would write other books after this one, *The St. Lawrence* (1942) and *Northern Farm* (1948), but *Herbs and the Earth* has an intensity that evokes the herbs themselves, as if, pressed between its pages, their aroma had seeped into the paper. Beston felt that the last paragraphs—his "Epilogue in Spring"— were the best he ever wrote.

Writing did not come easily to him. In composition, he might as well have been wrestling rocks onto a stoneboat. "There was always a kitchen table, a strong uncushioned chair, a mug filled with sharpened pencils, a large eraser and a pile of typewriter paper, more than half of which ended life on the floor," reported Elizabeth. His favorite place to write was atop the easternmost end of the house. From this attic, with its two small windows and a dormer, he could look down on the court, down on a pair of ancient apple and pear trees. Here he installed bookcases and a wood stove, and here he sometimes slept on stormy nights so that he might hear the force of the rain beating down on the slope of the roof. It was called the herb attic, from the bunches of dried herbs found hanging from the rafters. It is easy to imagine Henry Beston working here, safe between heaven and earth, surrounded by the ghosts of gardens past.

ROGER B. SWAIN, 1990

Foreword

P<small>ART</small> of the pleasure of writing this book has been
the help I have had from others. To my wife,
Elizabeth Coatsworth Beston, I would offer thanks
for an assistance so constant, so wise and so gener-
ously given that without it both manuscript and
author would still be missing in the garden. My
thanks are due to Mr. Harry E. Maule of Double-
day, Doran & Co., whose patience and courteous
interest have never varied while these slow pages
have been unfolding; to Mr. Henry M. Faxon,
whose kindness made possible a quiet study when
in town; to Miss Abbie Bradley and Mr. S. G.
Kimpton, gardener at Bradley Hill, for both herbs
and herbal advice; to Mrs. Mary B. Young for her
kind gift of many a New England rarity; to Mr.
and Mrs. F. Morton Smith for their winter hos-

pitality to my tenderer plants; to Miss Mabel
Davison for her unfailing encouragement; to my
mother for much good counsel, and to all the good
company of fellow herbalists who have helped me
with their wisdom and experience.

HENRY BESTON, 1935

OF HERBS AND THE EARTH

CHAPTER I

Of Herbs and the Earth

It was a pleasant fancy of the ancients that the lights of heaven, the sun and the moon, the errant planets and the military and ordered stars sang each his song as they moved in harmony upon their paths, ennobling thus the shell of space with music. Were mortal ears prepared to sustain such melodies, it was thought, one might chance to hear, at cloudless noon, in a high and quiet land, a sound of the great cry of the sun, and by night and the moon another music not of earth brushing against earth and the blood. In this celestial harmony what song, then, sang the earth? What vast and solemn music did this our planet make as turning upon its poles it wheeled through the universal void rolling up its cities to the sun and its fields down to the night? Was the sound but the uncon-

fused and primal voice of the planet welling for-
ever from its cores of stone, or did a sound of rivers
and many oceans, of leaves and immeasurable rain
mingle to make a mysterious harmony? And might
a listening god, perhaps, have heard echoes of
man, the shrilling of a plough turned from earth
into earth and stones, or a woman singing her
dream and her content?

It is only when we are aware of the earth and of
the earth as poetry that we truly live. Ages and
people which sever the earth from the poetic spirit,
or do not care, or stop their ears with knowledge
as with dust, find their veins grown hollow and
their hearts an emptiness echoing to questioning.
For the earth is ever more than the earth, more
than the upper and the lower field, the tree and the
hill. Here is mystery banded about the forehead
with green, here are gods ascending, here is benig-
nancy and the corn in the sun, here terror and
night, here life, here death, here fire, here the
wave coursing in the sea. It is this earth which is
the true inheritance of man, his link with his human past, the source of his religion, ritual and song,
the kingdom without whose splendor he lapses
from his mysterious estate of man to a baser world
which is without the other virtue and the other

integrity of the animal. True humanity is no inherent right but an achievement; and only through
the earth may we be as one with all who have been
and all who are yet to be, sharers and partakers of
the mystery of living, reaching to the full of human peace and the full of human joy.

Here in this pleasant arbor by the herbs, with
the grape overhead, and Basil in flower in the open
sun, here in this quiet varied with an early summer
sound of country birds, one may well muse awhile
on how the soul may possess and keep her earth inheritance. The age in which we live is curious and
bewildered; it is without a truly human past and
may be without a human future, and so abruptly it
came that one might imagine some cosmic spirit
or wayward daimon to have reached down of a
moment and plucked man by the hair. It has lost
the earth, but found (since the comfortable century
of philosophers in dressing gowns) a something
which it calls "nature," and of which it speaks
with enthusiasm and embalms in photographs. It
has lost as well the historic sense, the poignant and
poetic recognition of the long continuity of man,
that sense within our hearts which is moved by
a chance print in an old book of a countryman
ploughing with oxen beside ruins overgrown with

Fennel while to one side women clap cymbals together to calm the swarming bees.

A garden of herbs need be no larger than the shadow of a bush, yet within it, as in no other, a mood of the earth approaches and encounters the spirit of man. Beneath these ancestral leaves, these immemorial attendants of man, these servants of his magic and healers of his pain, the earth underfoot is the earth of poetry and the human spirit; in this small sun and shade flourishes a whole tradition of mankind. This flower is Athens; this tendril, Rome; a monk of the Dark Ages tended this green against the wall; with this scented leaf were kings welcomed in the morning of the world. Lovely and timeless, rooted at once in gardens and in life, the great herbs come to the gardener's hand our most noble heritage of green.

2

A garden is the mirror of a mind. It is a place of life, a mystery of green moving to the pulse of the year, and pressing on and pausing the while to its own inherent rhythms. In making a garden there is something to be sought, and something to be found. To be sought is a sense of the lovely and assured, of garden permanence and order, of human association and human meaning; to be found is beauty and that unfolding content and occupation which is one of the lamps of peace.

Gardens today seem often enough neither to seek nor to find. They make their effect, they attain a perfection, and they are curiously empty of human feeling or emotional appeal. In character they are pictures, painted with flowers as with oils, a color being touched in here and a blossom there till the canvas is ready to be seen. So purely an objective appeal, however, touches but one small and sometimes rather childish side of us, and the methods used to forward it tend to disrupt and destroy the garden sense of order and abiding loveliness. What human meaning have for us these tableaux in the crinoline grand manner, these huge scenes made from everything under the sun, or this use of boorish weeds in a new and unholy splendor, rarities as outlandish as a savage with a skewer through his nose, and old favorites turned hideous by a destruction of proportion? Surely a garden angel with a flaming sword is needed at the entrance of the catalogues! The gardening ancients were more wise. Flowers for them were but an aspect, an incidental loveliness of something near to man, living, and green. Plants were identities, presences to be lived

with, known, and watched growing; they were
shapes and habits of leaves, powers, fragrances, and
life-familiars. A sense of form gave the garden its
tranquillity, and one might hear there, in the full
of one's own peace, the serene footsteps of the year.

Even such a garden one still makes of herbs. A
plant of Balm, lifted from the June earth with its
beard of delicate roots, a bush of Thyme in flower
in the hot sun, Angelica rising in Gothic reeds
where the rich and level earth long stores its rain,
each of these is still a use, a potency, and a name. A
garden of herbs is a garden of things loved for
themselves in their wholeness and integrity. It is
not a garden of flowers, but a garden of plants
which are sometimes very lovely flowers and are
always more than flowers. It is a garden of color
seen as a part of garden life and not as its climax
and close, of the pleasures and refreshments of fragrance, of the fantasy and beauty of leaves, of the
joy of symmetry and design in nature, of that neglected delight to be found in garden contrasts and
harmonies of green. Sweet Bush Basil with its
plum-colored bracts and branches, green leaves
and tiny rose-white flowers, Sweet Basil with paler
green leaves and whitish florets, Wormwood green
and gray, Rue with its moonlight color of blue-

green, Clary with its fine spike of flowers, Marjoram of the enriching fragrance, how empty any
garden seems where they have no part! Where
there are herbs even the smallest of gardens has a
human past and is a human thing. But let there not
be too many herbs. The herbalist-to-be must a little
beware of a very old and very new confusion.

3

In the fifth scene of the fourth act of *All's Well
that Ends Well* there is already a dispute about
herbs. Says the Clown to Lafeu, speaking of the
Lady Helena, "Indeed, sir, she was the sweet marjoram of the salad or, rather, the herb of grace."
To which Lafeu replies, "They are not pot herbs,
you knave, they are nose herbs!" The Clown makes
answer that he is "no great Nebuchadnezzar" and
"has not much skill in grass," but he need not have
been apologetic. Nose herbs, pot herbs, salad herbs,
and healing herbs, who indeed shall say just which
is which and what is what when herbs are confus-
ingly now the one, now the other, now two or three
at once, now often enough all four? Bearing in
mind, however, that the use of herbs and the manner of this use is all a matter of taste, these group-
ings are helpful. One may well have one's own

corner of nose herbs, a corner of salad herbs, and all the others, but do not be aggrieved if a fellow gardener insists on rearranging everything and shows the captious spirit of Lafeu.

So much for one first confusion; a second is more fundamental. After all, what is an "herb"? In the new enthusiasm for the plants, there are those who will call anything an "herb" from a carrot to a night-blooming Cereus, and put it in their gardens. Horticulture and Botany, holding to a usage familiar to the King James, classify as "herbs" all plants which are not truly shrubs or trees; the dictionary calls an herb "a plant with a use." For lovers of herbs the word has another and much more living sense. In its essential spirit, in its proper garden meaning, *an herb is a garden plant which has been cherished for itself and for a use* and has not come down to us as a purely decorative thing. To say that use makes an herb, however, is only one side of the story. Vegetables, quasi-vegetables, herbal what-nots, and medicinal weeds are not "herbs" and never will be "herbs," for all the dictionaries. It is not use which has kept the great herbs alive, but beauty and use together. Clumsy food plants, curlicue salad messes and roots belong in the kitchen garden, in the *jardin potager*, and not with the herbs. They spoil the look of an herb garden, taking from it its inheritance of distinction; they confuse it; they destroy its unique atmosphere. Fancified horticultural varieties of floral herbs, near-herbs, and herbal relatives which have never been used as herbs—these, too, in general ought to be avoided, and if used, used of climatic necessity and used guiltily. No garden of herbs, moreover, should ever be intruded upon and prettified by non-herbal flowering plants, for such an intrusion destroys the unity and character of the garden, and if one wants bloom there are plenty of flowering herbs.

In making the garden, the emphasis should always rest on the beauty and character of the plants and never for a moment on the size and variety of the collections. Collections of herbs are interesting, often enormously so, but their rivalries end in their becoming much alike, and a fashionable scramble for rarities is not for the herbalist. A garden of herbs is something else, something a little apart from the need of numbering and counting and completing which is in the blood of our years, something which is of earth and of time and of magic and of peace. Let the garden be small and secret if it will, if it be made with understanding

it shall gather in its leaves that which has no garden bound or measure.

4

It is the very early morning, the house is not
yet awake, and in the garden refreshed with night
the bees are working in the herbs. The frailer
spikes of Hyssop sway under their weight, bend-
ing over like birches swung by boys; the Marjoram shakes and nods to their fumbling and climb-
ing and alighting; on the spikes of Basil they
thrust their whole heads into the larger flowers
and drive off newcomers with a buzz. Herbs bring
bees, bees with their immortal air of fable and the
Golden Age. Labiate flowers please them, for the
honeyed reward is generous and kept sheltered for
their taking.

Two great botanical families, the Labiatae or
Mint family and the Umbelliferae or Parsley family, share between them the majority of the familiar herbs. The Labiatae form a large and strongly
marked natural order especially abundant in the
Mediterranean region; to it belong the Mints and
the Sages, Basil and Balm, Marjoram and Rosemary and Lavender, Thyme, and a scatter more.
Plants of this family have commonly a squarish or

BASIL

four-angled stem, simple and opposite leaves, two-lipped flowers springing from the axils of leaves—sometimes arranging themselves there about the main stems in a pretty ring or wreath of bloom—and stamens by fours. Many are fragrant and aromatic, the odor having its origin in a volatile oil stored in tiny glands in the tissues of the leaves. Cereals apart, no single great group of plants has probably been of more service to mankind.

The Umbelliferae or Parsley family are again a large and valuable order. Here belong Lovage and Dill, Angelica, Parsley, Coriander, the Fennels and their like. In this order the individual flowers are small, even minute, and situated at the extremities of little stalks which branch out from the end of a stem (as in the too familiar Queen Anne's Lace) to form an "umbel." Leaves are seldom simple, but cut and divided; and their stalks tend to widen to a sheath at their base to clasp a hollow and rounded stem. Petals are five and stamens five, and the umbel as a whole is often white or yellowish. The aromatic elements are richest in the "seeds" or fruits, but occur as well in the substance of the plant. Umbelliferae vary a good deal in character, some of the species being among the most valuable food plants, others, like the Water-Hemlock, being poisonous.

Rue belongs to a family to which it has given its own name, the Rutaceae; Costmary, the Camomiles and the Artemisias are Composites; Borage and Comfrey belong to the Boraginaceae, and Burnet is of the Rose family.

Collecting herbs and the seeds of herbs is in itself a spirited and complete adventure. Seeds of the rarer herbs are not to be had at every corner. They hide in rare and fantastically interesting catalogues (blessèd for reading in bed), they lurk in the coat pockets of fellow herbalists, in *petites annonces* in French agricultural papers, in small envelopes from Switzerland numbered and hand-lettered in violet ink, and in teacups which have lost their saucers in the kitchens of old farms. In the British catalogues some are entered among the flowers, others in the general list of herbs; the French list a few among the *graines potagères*, a few with the flowers, and put the group as a whole in their medico-herbal muster of *plantes officinales et condimentaires*. So much for the unusual; as widely varied and delightful a garden as one could possibly wish can be made of seeds and plants easily procurable in America. Two or three of the larger firms now carry a good list of herb seeds and offer a selection of plants as well. One nursery makes of herbs a pleasant specialty.

Some day, perhaps, a lost herb or two will come again into human life. Who will bring us from Cretan hillsides an herb known to the Elizabethans and the Victorians, the ancient "Dittany" of the Greek Anthology (*Origanum Dictamnus*), a lovely and fragrant plant long ago dear to gods and to earth-wandering men?

5

Now sweeps a high wind over the farming land, shaking like a banner the fields which today await the mower, rushing wayward this way and that through the fruiting grass, all in a long lashing sound of wind and leaves. The sparrows who have come to glean in yesterday's greener stubble hold close to the earth, their brownish groups fly low, but the higher swallows are caught by the wind and soaring are blown about; the processional clouds move white. What winds shall blow, fall what lustral rains that the ancient sense of the beauty and integrity of the earth shall presently reawaken in the indifferent blood? Or must some great and furious storm (and such storms come) sweep clear the whole coast of the soul of man and restore him thus to his humanity? For man is of a quickening spirit and the earth, the strong, in-coming tides and rhythms of nature move in his blood and being; he is an emanation of that jour-neying god the sun, born anew in the pale South and the hollow winter, the slow murmur and the long crying of the seas are in his veins, the influ-ences of the moon, and the sound of rain beginning. Torn from earth and unaware, without the beauty and the terror, the mystery and ecstasy so right-fully his, man is a vagrant in space, desperate for the inhuman meaninglessness which has opened about him, and with his every step becoming some-thing less than man.

Peace with the earth is the first peace. Unto so great a mystery, to paraphrase a noble saying, no one path leads, but many paths. What pleasant paths begin in gardens, leading beside the other great mystery of nature, the mystery of the grow-ing green thing with its mute passion and green will. The day's high wind is walled off from the herbs, only the taller leaves stirring a little in the fringes of the gusts, the sun mounts from the south-east into the south, the black and yellow bees continue their timeless song. Beautiful and ancient presences of green, dear to man and the human spirit, let us walk awhile beside your leaves.

OF TEN GREAT HERBS

CHAPTER II

Of Ten Great Herbs

THE HOUSE IS PART of a farm and is old and country-like and painted a farmhouse red. It stands in the midst of fields on a hillside sloping east, with a lake below lying blue, and north and south are glimpses of the lake again over fields and trees, with hills and farms on the other side, and a far country of woods. On the side of the house overlooking the lake, there is a kind of rustic court, and this is not painted red but white, the change of color being a custom of the country. Two sides of this retreat are formed by the house itself with its windows and green blinds, a third is provided by an adjoined shed and lengthened by a copse of cherries, the fourth is open to the sunrise and the lake. It is a pleasant and Virgilian place, much loved of birds. One great old apple tree, beautiful in the antique manner, is the rustic guardian of the scene, attended to one side and a little below by an equally ancient pear. In this shelter of green and white, framed by the darker red, in this garden whose floor of grass slopes gently down to join the summer hay, I have my herbs.

There are two borders or beds or gatherings (I am not sure which word to use, for it is all quite unpretentious), one on the north by the cherries, which faces the southern sun, one on the west below an old foundation wall. I take a particular pleasure in this wall for the rustic beauty of its making, esteeming it a small masterpiece, no less, of the old New England art of stone, that folk-art of boulders and field rocks and fragments under the plough which can make even a cellar wall here a thing of beauty and integrity. Only oxen, I think, could have lifted these huge shales lying flat, or those weights of granite whose sides have so frosty a glint of quartz under their weathering. The wall is some eighteen feet long and about four high, and most of the stones are of an archaic greenish gray. Things do well at its foot, for they have its shelter and the moisture it holds in the earth. There Balm lives, growing as Balm should grow in a mass of flourishing, close-gathered green, Apple-

mint made of more interest with a plant or two
of its variegated form, Bee-Balm white and red
standing close against a corner of the wall, Bergamot Mint with its French and eighteenth-century
elegance, English Pennyroyal, the prostrate form,
creeping out from under a stone, and a few small
plants of Dill. In the longer border facing south
grows a whole "tussiemussie" of plants which have
filled out and grown together to make a pleasant
and unstudied show. Here are Hyssop and Basil, a
corner shrub of Southernwood, a clump of kitchen
Sage, Pot Marjoram and Lavender (that European-minded plant), Virgil's Cerinthe with its
yellow blossoms, Spike Vervain (to the classical
peoples the most sacred of all growing things), a
plant or two of the Biblical "Hyssop" which is a
Marjoram (*Origanum Maru*) sent to me by a schol-
ar in Palestine, a good clump of Costmary and its
botanical relative Camphor Balsam, Lovage and
Woundwort, Valerian and Comfrey, a noble plant
of Absinthe Wormwood, and even, O happy rarity,
that preëminent plant of folklore, the screaming
Mandrake Root. The Thymes are by themselves,
and to one side and out from the shadow of the
northern wall stands that ancient potency, a bank
of Rue. A border facing north I give over to a

white Astilbe and a very unpretending show of white and yellow annuals.

I write down only those herbs which come to my mind, not wishing to begin a catalogue. Counting almost as I write, with that separate part of the mind which seems to do so well by us at a pinch, I find that I have at the moment forty-three herbs. Of a number of these I keep but one strong plant, which is enough, of others two or three, of those which are used a good deal, six and more. It is a mistake, I think, to have more than forty or fifty herbs at any one time, for the plants are, as I have said, individuals and presences, and to overplant means a loss of that civilized pleasure of growing a beautiful and interesting thing and getting to know it well. The hideous delight of the early twentieth century in masses and numbers was a touch of the insect mind, a thing tent caterpillars would have perfectly understood. My own method is to have a definite group of favorites, mostly established perennials, and with this group as a foundation to try a few new herbs every year or some delightful old ones all over again. A good way to begin a garden is to start with a representative selection and let the garden grow naturally from these when the garden and the gardener's mind are ready. But I had best get to my own notion of such a list.

I call the selection, you notice, "ten great herbs" and not "the ten great herbs," which title would provoke an herbal Armageddon of otherwise peaceable and philosophical gardeners, and conjures up the vision of a field strewn with trowels, and abandoned plants and fugitives. I have come to choose these ten because they are all pleasant to work with in the earth, because they are old and famous plants, and because as a group they give a good idea of what herbs can bring to gardening and living. Basil begins the list, then follow in order Marjoram, Balm, Bergamot Mint or French Bergamot (*Mentha Citrata*), Sage, Hyssop, Rue, Spike Vervain, Lovage, and Lavender. Complete cultural directions, the popular and the foreign names, the matter of native American herbal allies, and so forth, I keep for a convenient and separate table. What I should like to give here is a sense of the herb itself and the impression it makes as a plant and a familiar.

2

We have had three weeks, almost a month, of rainless August heat. Last night, soon after the lamps were lit, I saw the first small drops on the outer darkness of the panes, and presently from under the kitchen floor the faint whisper of water trickling into the cistern could be heard in the silence of the room. This morning, the whole landscape is renewed, and the garden has its own good smell again of rain-wet earth and leaves. The green life of earth is a deeper life than we know, having its roots in touch with the waters under the earth, with those rills flowing unseen out of ledges deep in the ground. It is when the garden is unable to drink its fill from beneath, when the living ascent of moisture from the deeper earth to root earth is impeded, that plants begin to take on that lifeless air and curious, lifeless feel which surface water never quite dispels. In the court a woodpecker flies into the apple tree, making his way through the leaves without a sound; trees, sky, grass, house, herb garden, and flowers all shine together in a sun with a peaceable air, and walking out to see, I notice that the fine-leaved plants are still comfortably drenched whilst those with simpler and entire leaves are already dry.

In a corner by the wall, a plant of purple Basil stands quite by itself, and with washed and shining leaves makes vital alliance with the light. No herb.

is more generous of its fragrance, and this morning
the rich, clove-like odor hangs above the plant
like a small cloud unseen, mingling its refreshment
with the good odor of the earth. You may see the
wells of essential fragrance on the under side of the
oval leaves, where they appear as a cloud of pin-
point dots. I have both kinds of Basil here, the
Purple or Bush Basil and the Sweet or Green. Basil
is an accommodating plant. Crowd it into a pot or
nook of earth and it will not sicken or go queer,
shooting off a long ungainly stem to this side and
an abortive nubbin to the other, but will intelligently and interestingly readjust its whole scale,
reducing stem and leaf and flower in one proportion. In the garden, too, the herb will give you
about what you permit, either a pretty little bush-
like form with purple wands and purple bracts and
lighter flowers, or a handsome plant which is one
of the most distinguished of herbal presences.

A fine plant of Basil is first of all a composition
in interesting colors, a Tyrian or red plum-purple
and a very living green. The purple is in the
branches and the stems, the bracts above the flowers and the tufted rosettes of growth-to-be at the
ends of the stems; the green is in the leaves. (Plants
grown indoors stay much more green.) These are

colors of India of which the Basils used as herbs are natives, a liking for pink and green being traditional in Indian art and life. The growth of the plant is strong, vital, and orderly (it is a perennial treated as an annual), and my large plants with their trunklike stems and rounded growth above often remind me of miniature and symmetrical trees. The French, with their keen sense of form and feeling for fragrance, grow Basil as an ornamental plant as well as an herb, and have developed a dwarf variety of the Green for use in their rather formal gardening.

The Basils I grow stand nearly two feet tall. The flower "spikes" of the Purple, though they are only purple stems (sometimes branches) wreathed like a maypole with a series of purple bracts and rose-whitish flowerets, are nevertheless unusual and full of character. Green Basil, too, is an excellent plant, of a simpler and more open growth than its companion, and has white flowers and green bracts and leaves of a paler, blonder green. In this garden I give a few plants of the Purple all the room they need and mass a dozen plants of the Green in the general border. Culturally, the plant is a bequest of the Hellenistic world, an herb of the warmer climates of the Roman Empire, and has

been known and used from the earliest times as a
condiment, a fragrance, and a medicine. No herb
of all the garden is more used here by the household; it goes into every nosegay, into the salads,
into everything made with tomatoes, an alliance
with these last having been fore-ordained. The
Green is the best for general culinary use. The
name of the herb comes from the Greek noun
meaning "a king," and was perhaps given for the
Tyrian purple it assumes. During the Dark Ages
Basil seems to have been somewhat lost sight of in
the West, but with the Renaissance it came into
its own again and recaptured the garden and the
imagination.

Whenever I walk among the herbs at noon, at
that hour when a Spanish country saying will have
it that the forces of the earth are at their exaltation
of power, I can never pass one of the great Basils
in the sun without a thought beginning there of
the fantastic wonder of the whole green life of
earth. Pivoted upon its share of soil, potent with
its intensity of living, symmetrical and predetermined to symmetry, a fine plant of Basil is a form,
a gathering together of that mysterious vitality of
green whose veins draw up the earth itself, and
whose impulse of life is the other side of that

rhythm of life stirring with us in our blood. What a passion for life plants reveal, what a body and desire of life dwell in the dark of roots and the hunger under the earth! What will they not endure to live and bear, not surmount of caprice and outrage, of attack and disaster, if they can but lift one flower from the ruin. What a sense of will there is in the vine, in the groping of the tendril, in the ultimate seizure and adherence! Denied the animal resource of flight, an intensity of life is their ark and weapon; fixed upon earth they can but fight death with life. We are not conscious enough in our human world of this other shaping of life beside us, taking little account of its presence and its ways, yet without such an awareness our thought of life must remain a thing of our own firesides where none see beyond the flame.

With Sweet Marjoram one comes to an herb which is a study in the little elegancies and niceties of proportion. It is of the true Sweet or Knotted Marjoram that I write, *Origanum Marjorana* in the Latin. Not a tiny herb at all, or one which grows primly, no other herb that I know has quite the same appeal of scale, the same small, fragrant propriety.

I have five plants here growing by a little cliff of whitish granite which is the side of a stone continuing the greater wall. They came from a nursery, for this Marjoram is again a perennial treated as an annual, and I like to have well-started plants to put into place in June. All summer long I have watched them growing from thrifty seedlings into charming and very civil little plants of a loosely bushy nature, plants with somewhat red and delicately woody stems, the longer ones curving out and up from the roots, each close trimmed with opposite clusters of small and oval leaves. At the tops of the stems and in the axils of the higher leaves have now appeared the curious and pretty buds which give the plant one of its familiar names. These are the "knots," four-sided cones or miniature thyrsi of green whose walls of tiny overlapping scales thrust from between them the specks of white that are the flowers. The Elizabethans thought of them as resembling the heads of boys, and they do, in a way, recall such a group of clustered heads as one sees looking out from the corners in the old religious canvases. The word "knot" itself is undoubtedly a memory of some device of the old needlework or embroidery which the buds chanced to recall.

A neat and pretty plant, Sweet Marjoram is perhaps the most human and amiable of the smaller herbs. It is a plant easy to care for and easy to grow; it thrives in any good garden soil, withstands the vagaries of weather, and is plagued by no thief of leaves. In domestic use, it is the base of a Marjoram vinegar which is a pleasant deputy for the Tarragon, and a few leaves—not too many, for the taste can have a small bitterness—go with the Basil into salads.

The other Marjoram of which the garden should always have its share (for it is one of the best and prettiest of the floral herbs) is "Pot Marjoram," call it in Latin what you will. This is a much heavier, larger plant, which grows to be a strong, branching clump two feet high covered with dark leaves and abundant clusters two or three inches wide of purplish flowers which bloom all the summer long. I find it one of the most sturdy and resistant of all the garden plants. It is quite easily grown from seed, though what you will get depends on the nursery and your seedsman. It may be *Origanum Onites*, an old perennial plant from the Caucasus, or a horticultural variety of the wild Marjoram of Europe and the British Isles, *Origanum Vulgaris*, a hardy perennial there and a reasonably hardy one here. Practically all the plants I have seen lately are nursery strains of the *Vulgaris*. Whatever or whichever it may be, "Pot Marjoram" is a plant for every herbalist and every garden of herbs.

In making their gardens and choosing their flowers, the ancients had a profound feeling for the lovely quality of fragrance. Mile upon mile beyond Augustan Rome lay the rose gardens which provided the city with its favorite flower; the Dark Ages saved for us the herbs, keeping alive in their vast and unpeopled ruin such plants as Spearmint and Parsley, which are so human and old that they are not to be found in nature; the Elizabethan flower and herb lists were an old-fashioned floral vase of pleasant smells. For fragrance is indeed what the past well knew it to be, a refreshment and a strength, a sweet and human pleasure, an exorciser of demons from the body and the besieged and troubled spirit. Subtlest of influences, touching the emotion directly, asking nothing from the mind, it not only wakes in us an emotion of place, but summons up as well a poignant emotion of ourselves as we were in time and the place remembered. The odor of a ploughed field in the spring is like a hand laid upon the heart, having in it all the beauty, the poignancy, and the tenderness of earthly living, all the poetry of the melancholy and ecstasy of spring, of the branch, the new leaf and the warm wind, and the sinking of some last great and solitary winter star.

Part of our delight in the good fragrance of herbs comes from their being in relation to mankind. For some odors are subhuman, being contrived and distilled for insects and such small deer, and others are overhuman, being meant for genii, so overpowering are they and cloying. The fragrance of herbs is a thing of the human scale which lies between. Like all other manifestations of life, it is a thing of change, the scents varying subtly with the growth of the plants, the time of the year, and even the time of the day. There are herbs which are best in daytime, and others which are best in the early morning when even the dew upon their leaves is fragrant. Now and then it comes to pass that an herb will have one fragrance in one part of the garden and quite another elsewhere (Hyssop does this), and plants of the same herb all growing together may have marked individualities of odor. With some herbs, Rue, for instance, there is an underfragrance which is almost a separate thing.

A nosegay of herbs in a room makes no insist-
ence, but once it has the attention it holds it, and
it is beyond all customary experience refreshing.
The fragrances are real ones, and not, as so many
things are with us, manufactured essences one re-
move from life. That inauspicious suggestion lurk-
ing in modern perfumes of the animal mingled
with the floral, as if someone had led a musk-ox
through a bed of Nicotianas, is with herbs cleansed
from the nose. Bouquets of herbs, moreover, stay
fresh an amazingly long time and do not befoul
the water. Such a bouquet, too, is always a little
more than a nosegay, it is a collection of the beliefs,
the wisdoms and the fantasies of our kind remembered in green.

Of all herbal fragrances there is none to my
mind more pleasant than that of Sweet Marjoram,
of that plant which the French call *"Marjollaine
à Coquille"* and put with keepsakes and add to
salads.

A swarm of bees leaving the hive, said Virgil,
rush like a dark cloud to "sweet waters and leafy
shades," and there must the bee-keeper hasten
to lay "bruised Balm" and Honeywort that the
sweet odors may detain them. The plant he first

recommends, giving it a Latin form of its Greek name, is "Melisphylla" or "the Bee-Leaf" and the great first-century herbalist Dioscorides adds that bees do indeed delight in the herb, which is something similar to the "Black Horehound" and has leaves with a lemon smell. This is no other than the Balm of our own gardens, now Latinized anew as *Melissa Officinalis*, and variously called in English, Balm, Lemon Balm, Sweet Balm, and Balm Gentle. No plant of the garden has a better classical pedigree, and there is even a possible mention in the *Odyssey*. To the ancients a plant of fragrance and a companion of bees, to the Middle Ages a fragrance and the source of a healing balsam ("Balm" being but "Balsam" made short), Balm is now a time-honored presence whose medical fame has waned, but whose standing as a fragrance and an herb of gardens is perhaps higher than ever before.

Though it is pleasant to work with plants in a garden and bring them to their best, discovering what things help or hinder them, it is also pleasant to have at hand plants which may be trusted to do their best quite by themselves. I know of no plant better able to do this than Balm. Sturdy, hardy, and vigorous, strongly made and strongly growing, it tends to its own green affairs, holding the fortress of its soil with a great bush of rootlets buried and ramified in a large ball of earth, retaining its grasp, yet not trespassing. Keeping, it would seem, to the *via media* of classical tradition, it avoids weakness on the one hand and strength become thievish on the other, a habit which makes it a particularly pleasant and dependable herb. It is a genuine perennial, and emerges from its root in the spring with a leading stalk or two, one of which tends to become the main stalk of the summer plant, thrusting out axillary branches as it grows which in their turn trim themselves with shorter branches and smaller leaves. The grown plant is not so much a bush as a lodge of leafy branches, some erect, others sloped off, all crisp and clean, all fragrant with a good and earthy smell of lemon. The white flowerets stand in the axils of specialized stems, appearing in calices interestingly arranged as a fan, and the buds are ivory.

Balm is so pleasant a plant and is used so much here during the summer as a green fragrance in the house that I have a whole bed of it in the garden which I allow to grow together in a not too crowded mass of green. Quantities of it were used in Elizabethan England to scour the furniture and give a pleasant smell when notables were expected; there is a reference to the practice in *The Merry Wives of Windsor*, Act V, Scene v. It is easy to grow from seed though a little slow to germinate, and the young plants well placed come into full growth their first year. Broken light and shade and a place in moist earth are the best things for Balm, or a situation in an east border with limited hours of sun; direct heat and dry soil will but dwarf it. The herb is normally from twelve to eighteen inches tall. I space the plants which go into the bed eight inches apart and allow single plants established outside to have a full square foot of soil. The herb is occasionally come upon as a garden escape in old counties in New England and Virginia.

I find few things in a garden of more curious interest than the relation of light and shade to the shapes and surfaces of leaves. Of the color of leaves and the primary relation of light to that color I shall not speak here, for it is the difference in the reflection of the light and the adaptation of the surface to the intricacies of light and shade I would rather call to the gardener's musing mind. A leaf is a subtle thing, being far more than a casual first appearance of form and color and light. There are leaves which by their shape hold the

BALM

light as in a cup, others which let it flow from them almost as rain might flow; there are leaves which are mirrors reflecting the sun from a glaze of varnished green, and others which are delicate transparencies through whose living screen the sun passes with a strange and lovely tempering. Here in the garden I have these and a hundred other variations, but it is by the leaves of Balm that I find myself pausing when I chance to visit the garden in the morning when the plant faces the eastern sun. It is a simple leaf, not large when averagely well grown, measuring perhaps two inches from base to point, egg-shaped more or less, and scalloped in a descending rhythm to its narrowing end. Very short, whitish hairs rise from its upper surface, thinly sown and often next to invisible, and the usual color is a greenish yellow-green. So far, perhaps, it might be any of a thousand leaves: what gives it a peculiar interest is the bold texture and the deep indentations of the veins which make the surface an intricate pattern in relief, each minute enclosure being raised to the higher light of the sun, each vein being sunken to an actual channel of shade. It is the sense of the network of veining (so favorite a device of nature) being again a network of shade, which holds my attention as I walk. For the shadow is melted there when the sun is overhead, and the veins emptying of darkness become but lines, yet swiftly the veining shadow gathers again, being never entirely absent somewhere on the plant. But all nature is full of these subtleties of light, and nowhere are they to be better seen than on the wings of birds and the surfaces of leaves.

3

This noontime, while the men were resting from the mowing, I saw something very curious happen in the field. The hay had been cut upon our upper slopes and lay drying in the stubble, and further down where the grass had been cut a day before, stood a haycock loosely piled. Suddenly between me and the glimpse of the team unharnessed and our neighbors eating dinner in the shade came a small and local whirlwind which crossed the road like a presence, and began its journey down the slope, picking up the hay. The air in its path was presently a wild shower of new hay tossed fifty and sixty feet high, more flying up as the vortex grew in its motion down the hill. It then took the top from the pile, scattered it over the field, and swept on across the uncut lower slope to the lake, dark-

ened it with a catspaw path and vanished like
djinn from a bottle halfway to the other side.
Straws and towsles of hay drifted down from the
sky, lodging in the leaves of the apple trees and
strewing all the nearer road, and presently all was
as it had been or nearly so, and the farm bell rang
for the noonday meal.

Autumn is familiarly the season of color, winter is the season of form, spring the season of texture, and summer the season of motion. Leaves and
branches move, casting shadows which move beneath them, the long grass ripples and bends, the
brooks slide and divide about the stone, the invisible and warmer wind is in itself a motion more
intricate than the winter's front of rushing cold.
Today, however, save for the djinn which lately
troubled the field, a true country peace hangs in
the hot sunlit air, and from the garden I follow
with my ear the rattling click of the mowing ma-
chine to the end of its swale, hearing then the
shout and ho! to the horse and the sound again
beginning.

In each far corner of the bed of Balm, its leaves
mingling with the Balm yet raised above it, stands
an herb whose essential quality can best be ren-
dered by saying that it is the most feminine of all

the herbs. It is Bergamot Mint (*Mentha Citrata*) or Lemon Mint, sometimes called French Bergamot to distinguish it from the true Bergamot, which is Italian. In texture this herb is the most beautiful of the mints, being smooth and elegant of leaf, the whole plant, indeed, having very much a finished and a measured air. Its leaves are smaller than the leaves of Balm, its neighbour, and the new growth at the ends of the main stems and the axillary branches makes flat and patterned rosettes firmly attached and colored from below with a bronzy purple staining through with the light to the upper surfaces. Delicate, valid, and in a certain way elaborate, the herb is in general form an outward-growing and loosely symmetrical clump which reaches a height of some eighteen or twenty-four inches. A great favorite in eighteenth-century France, when taste and fashion were of feminine inspiration, it was often included in the flower paintings of the time for the sake of its leaves flushed purple under green and the French violet of the flowers. It still flourishes there in the gardens of old provincial country houses, honored both for its fragrance and for its use in the making of liqueurs.

As a garden plant, Bergamot Mint needs moist

soil and broken shade—more or less what Balm requires—and though reasonably hardy it should have some protection through the winter. Plants are purchasable from American dealers.

Because the violet spikes of Bergamot Mint are not in a conventional sense considered "garden flowers" I find myself pausing a little at the phrase to weigh its meaning. A garden flower, I suppose, is a flower planted for its beauty, or more truly for its aspects of beauty, for we must take our garden pleasure now in a color, now in a texture, now in a form, now in a fragrance, now in a combination or a partial combination of these elements. The single dahlias blooming at the kitchen door are an example of my meaning, they have texture, an arresting and lovely color, and a country vigor, and with these they must say their all. An ideal garden flower therefore might seem to be one in which all aspects of beauty were harmoniously united, but the truth is that many very beautiful flowers do not move us at all. Leaving the physical aside, there is another world of values by whose standards we consciously and unconsciously judge the fitness of a flower, remaining unmoved by it unless it awaken some human emotion, stirring some old memory or touching and arousing the imagi-

nation. The values of the gardener's spirit are as
great as the values of the gardener's eye, and it is
because they have been a little put aside that the
vulgar curse of giantism has so descended upon us,
and gardens have fallen into so impersonal a rut.
The lovely spikes of Bergamot Mint are not large,
and they have not that importance proportional to
their leaves which flowers often seem to need, but
they are ringed with color to their tapering cones,
and are fragrant with the fragrance of the herb.
They do not *sauter aux yeux*, but they have charm
and the power to move the mind, for these same
delicate spikes have stood in floral vases in the great
eighteenth-century rooms, and heard the urbane
delight of music, seen candles brought in to light
the brocades and the sword hilts and the jewels,
and heard the sound of women's voices discussing
the policies of kings.

A little in the shelter of the robust Pot Marjoram and placed near the Lavender stands an herb
with as interesting a leaf as the garden shows. In
color it is a dull, unvarnished green; in form, an
elongated and tapering oval held on a stalk its
own length; in texture it is pebbled like the skin
of a chameleon. I know of no other leaf which by

pure texture gives so curious a suggestion of a kingdom on the other side of nature. Touched with
both beauty and strangeness, the leaf is a thing to
catch the eye and to prompt a question; it is the
leaf of Garden Sage, the *Salvia Officinalis* of the
botanists.

I had thought when I put the plant into the garden that friends would quickly recognize it there,
but only a few have done so. Apparently Garden
Sage as a plant is not as well known as its virtues
and uses indicate. Yet the herb is one of the greater
ancients, having never lapsed from favor, and its
pebbled leaf alone would make it an interesting
thing. In its native region of the Mediterranean
littoral of Europe, Sage is a true shrub; north of
its range it is a garden perennial, throwing out
new branches and branchlets every year from the
woody base of its stalks. Well-established plants
are so easily to be had from dealers that I usually
buy mine, taking care to put in a few new plants
every other year, for Sage, like many perennials of
its type, tends to run out. As a garden plant, I find
it one of the most satisfactory of herbs. It is strong-
growing, resistant to weather, unplagued of insects, has something of a flower, and is picturesque
in color and manner of growth. I put my plants

SAGE

in fairly close together to get a mass effect of the curious leaves, standing them in the full and open light. Sage never looks better, I think, than when I come upon it in the early morning and find the pebbled leaves silvered over with a summer dew. In its way there is nothing more quietly individual in all the garden. Several forms and varieties of the genuine herb are accessible (a form with reddish younger leaves being familiar in England), but American dealers generally keep to one kind, a vigorous, large-leaved type well suited to our climate. In earlier times the magnificent annual Sage *Salvia Horminum* was also used in Europe as an herb, and seeds of it and its decorative hybrids are still offered in French and English flower catalogues; I have known it to be called "Annual Clary."

Whatever Sage may have been in the past, and its Latin name shows that it was a plant of saving and healing, it is now essentially a culinary herb. Its place is beside the spices and the flavors, the condiments and the relishes for which men have risked their lives, fought romantical battles, and committed every form of piracy and sea-rascality known or imaginable in the seventeenth century. What a curious history could be written of the

great spices and the changing tastes in food! The
herbs provided cookery with its earliest flavors,
and to these the Romans added the Eastern spices
(for they had them as they had many of our rarer
fruits and table luxuries), experimenting in the
sated years of the empire with flavor upon flavor,
even adding animal essences to their more fantastic
dishes. With the breakdown of the trade routes
and the universal poverty, the Dark Ages returned
to a native European cookery with simpler flavors, doing what they could with herbs and the
clove of garlic, with the onion and the spoonful of
wine. It was the Renaissance which took to spices
again, having rediscovered them and the East, and
the Elizabethans with their usual exuberance filled
with spice everything which appeared upon their
tables. One familiar dish remains of their cookery,
the very typical Elizabethan mixture of meat,
spices, apples, brandy, and what-not, which is the
mincemeat of mince pie. Though herbs were never
entirely disused or disdained, it was the French
and the Latins, generally, it would seem, who rediscovered and properly reëstablished them in po-
lite cookery during the seventeenth and most experimental of centuries. Sage was one of the first
kitchen herbs of the new dispensation, having

been forsaken by medicine, and with the canisters it has stood ever since, an amiable household presence to this hour.

When the heat of some long summer day has followed the sun behind the pasture hill, when the glare has gone and the hour of the garden hose and the watering pot approaches with the dusk, when the whole of nature surrounding the gardener as he works is vibrating with a heavy-laden summer immediacy and profusion of life and there is a moment's flutter of birds in the apple tree, when the lake, the garden, and the hill are each released from the weight and the splendor of day, how pleasant it is to be busy with the earth in this place of green! Here the first coolness comes, welling from the earth and fragrant with herbs, the odors mingling and strengthening as the gardener stirs the beautiful and timeless leaves, here gathers the first quiet of the coming evening, that quiet of summer and beginning night which overlies the fruitful tension of the earth. The herbs tonight approach their summer best, the great umbels of the Lovage breaking into yellow bloom, the tops of the Borage opening their pendant stars, and the

spikes of Hyssop like Aaron's Rod ringing themselves with flowers.

Be it the close of a burning afternoon or some
cold daybreak of the earlier fall, the Hyssop takes
earth and its weather as they come. The garden
has no more quietly dependable and satisfactory
border plant. A native of southern Europe, and an
"evergreen" of the Mediterranean type, it makes
no protest at months here under the snow, and
emerges sound and vital in the spring; neither dry
weather nor the autumn rains in the least bedevil
it, and it can be transplanted as casually as one
moves a chair. Yet it exhibits none of the truly
daimonic fury of vitality stirring in many a hardy
plant; it manages things in the other way, living
from a deep reserve of endurance and vital power.
In appearance an older plant of Hyssop is a kind
of little, rounded sub-shrub somewhere from nine
to twelve inches high, with branches bushing out
from the root and growing erect, most of them
branching again. The small willow-shaped leaves
occur in whorls spaced along the stalk, each whorl
accompanied by axillary tufts of leaflets, and the
axillary flowerets borne on the higher spikes are
sparks of a vivid violet blue—a white-flowered

form being also in cultivation. Younger plants are herbaceous in nature and less bushy in appearance.

As I have elsewhere written, the odor of the herb varies, it being one of the herbal and medicinal smells more than a fragrance, but the general impression of it is of something clean and aromatic with perhaps a very mellowed touch of turpentine. This odor of turpentine (the word is all that is left of the Terebinth tree of poetry) and a lemon fragrance appear again and again in nature. The medicinal suggestion is not misleading, for an old-fashioned syrup made of honey mixed with an infusion of Hyssop leaves and flowers is still in domestic use as a cure for coughs and colds. Hyssop should have a pleasant and sunny situation and the usual good border care. It is the plant we should use for some of the uses of Lavender, for it looks well with other things planted against a wall, and can be used as a pretty and rustic edging for beds along a walk. I have my plants in a row about halfway back in the border with young bushes of Rue before them and Spike Vervain behind.

Hyssop is a pleasant and useful plant, and one with which newcomers to herbs will quickly feel at home. Gardeners with herbs grow into a very living relation with the garden they tend. Their plants are individualities, some more than others, and they come to know them leaf by leaf and quality by quality, taking pleasure in them for the beauty and interest of their garden lives, and content to wait for their changes and manifestations. Impatience does not beset them, for their herbs are of interest from the moment they appear in spring, lifting their fragrance and beauty of leaf out of still another winter; they are willing that their plants shall take their time, well aware that here any flower is but a part of the cycle of beauty. It is from this equable temper of gardener and garden that the living relation between them which can be so subtle and profound can best arise. Only by some such imponderable bond may the response which certain plants make to certain people be explained, the debt on the other side being even more intangible but no less real. When the bond is truly living, both shall be sustained, and in return for the human cherishing, something of earth's patience and instinct of life, something of the peace of gardens, shall find its way into the flowing of the blood.

There is a fine garden scene in Shakespeare's *Richard II*, Act III, Scene IV. It would seem to be

about the middle of the morning, and Richard's
Queen is wandering with her ladies in the Duke
of York's garden at Langley, sorrowful for the
trouble of the times, and uncertain where to turn.
The head gardener enters with his men, bidding
them bind up the "dangling apricocks" and "root
away the noisome weeds," and as he and his fellows
discuss the garden they point from it a moral of
the state of the kingdom, and it is presently said
that the King has been deposed. Overhearing the
news, the Queen bursts into a passion of angry
grief, reproaching the gardener for tidings so un-
welcome, and sweeps away, followed by her attendants. When she is gone the gardener soliloquizes,
stirred to pity, and ends by saying that where she
stood he'll set a bank of Rue, "Rue even for ruth,"
"in the remembrance of a weeping Queen."

It is only in the world of English speech that
this dark and potent plant has come to have an
association with thoughts of sorrow and regret,
and it is all due to a resemblance in the sounds of
words. To the Romans, who probably brought the
plant into England, the herb was "Ruta," and the
name being retained and gradually simplified to
"Rewe," a notion of sympathetic identity between
the dark leaf and the emotion of "ruth" or com-

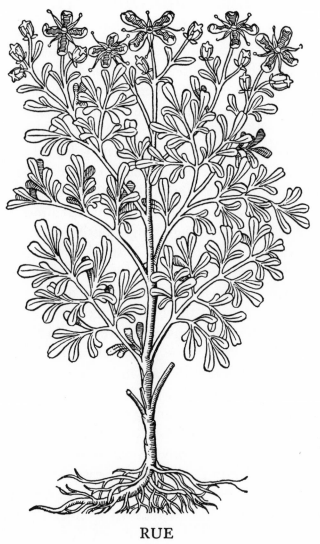

RUE

passionate sorrow formed itself in the popular mind. Elsewhere in Europe it remained much what it was in Roman times, an herb and a potency ancient as man himself, a remedy all-valuable and a little dangerous. That Rue could be poisonous to certain skins was known to Pliny and the older herbalists, and I give the warning for what it is worth, for I have never chanced to see a case. No herb has in its way kept a closer alliance with mankind. The ancient nations of the Mediterranean had it from their beginnings, passing it on to the Greeks and the Romans; it stood in the gardens of Charlemagne; it rose dark among the tenth-century herbs; the magic and medicine of the Middle Ages and the Renaissance both acknowledged it as a power; its roots are deep in the folklore of the West. The beautiful name "Herb of Grace" which it still bears in literature is an echo of the times when a brush of it was used to sprinkle the people at the beginning of the mass—the "asperges" ceremony of the Roman liturgy.

Were it ever to come to pass that I could have but two herbs in the garden, Rue would always be the other. There is nothing in the garden more curiously beautiful in its own manner than this plant. Once again, it is a southern European herb, shrubby in growth and a native of its region's poorer soils, in its own countries tending to keep its color through the year. In the north it grows to be about a foot high, sometimes a little more, coming up each spring like Sage from the trimmed, woody bases of last year's perished stalks. The new growth is dense, the small clumps compact, and in June and July the closely grown tops star over with cruciform yellow flowers like painted amulets. The leaf is as singular as the flower. It is a leaf of fern-like divisions with many rounded lobes, the lesser leaflets sloping in to the central stalk, its substance smooth, somewhat thickened and almost opaque. In color the plant is like nothing else in the garden, for it is a dark and somber tone of blue green lightened with a silvering of gray.

I have a few plants of Rue in the border, and a whole bank of it growing by itself in silhouette against the lake. The quality of the herb is best seen when it is given a place of its own; it likes good soil and the sun, and winters best where the drainage is adequate, for the cord-like roots go deep.

Mysterious in color and strange of leaf, potent, ancient, and dark, Rue is the herb of magic, the symbol of the earthly unknown, of the forces and wills behind the outer circumstance of nature, of natural law suddenly made subject to power. It was with magic that men first sought to control or thwart the wills and the natures of things, calling a cloud with words and forcing back the blood with incantations. Something, indeed, of the great magic of fertility which underlies and overlies religion still lingers on the earth, there to endure till the last child be born and the last field be sown. The instruments of so mighty an art were sometimes humble and small (for magical virtues may choose strange habitations) and power often dwelt among the herbs, in the leaf of Rue, in the spikes of Vervain, there to be plucked and used by the initiate to hold the unknown in the grasp of the known. "Canst thou bind the sweet influences of Pleiades or loose the bonds of Orion?" The herbs are used for magic no more, but the unaccountable remains, like a sound of hidden water in a cavern we have searched from end to end with lights.

4

Here in the North, summer comes earlier to its close, and the sign of the turn of the year is less a first thinning and coloring of leaves than a first great drenching rain. Beginning at night, the small crepitation of the rain wakes the sleeper in the attic chamber, who listens awhile for joy of the sound and is again asleep, the gray morning is confused with rain, and all day long the wind flattens against the house, blowing across the lake from the east and the distant sea. When the weather breaks and the sun again shines, it is autumn. The trees are still in apparent summer leaf, but the substance of the leaves is dry for all the storming, and enough have been blown down to reveal a gleam of the lake through green which was once a wall. It is the lovelier, brighter light of autumn which gilds this seeming summer, the lake is a brighter blue, and a new quiet has come upon the land.

Of what plant it was which first became an ally of man, who shall speak with authority? Was it the wheat with its sacred spear or barley of the dry and fruitful whisper or a wildling perhaps tried for a season and returned again to companions of the grass? One by one, now taken from the wood, now from the river mire, now seized from the barrens and the stone, the plants came into human life, and among the first were the herbs. Was the earliest to come perhaps a magical thing, some potency of earth mysteriously united with powers regnant in nature but not yet become as gods? There grows in the garden here a very ancient plant which has been a part of the magic and religion of the most diverse European cultures, in England being a sacred plant of the Druids, in Scandinavia a plant of the priests of Thor, in Greece and Rome a plant so holy that no other might be used to brush the altars of Olympian Jove. Yet it is not a stately plant but a quite simple one, almost a thing of the roadsides and the fields. *"Hierobotane"* the Greeks called it, the "Holy Plant"; and *"Herba Sacra"* the Romans. To us it is Spike or Herbal Vervain, the *Verbena Officinalis* of Linnæus.

Whatever list of annuals I make for the garden, this ancient herb is sure to be written down. It has enough garden presence of a rustic kind to justify its inclusion, being in no way boorish or uncivil, and it is easy to start from seed and easy to grow. A thriving plant reaches a height somewhere between eighteen and thirty inches, branching loosely as it rises, the leaves being variable in shape but commonly three-lobed, the flowers or florets purple specks borne irregularly on groups of spikes which are elongated and tapering cones. The bluer florets of its native counterpart, *Verbena Hastata*, a taller hardy perennial, are sometimes seen here in waste places, and the plant itself is now being offered by dealers in native things. Seed of *V. Officinalis*, which is still used in domestic medicine as a help in the early stages of colds and fevers, are to be had, as far as I know, only from European firms. The herb is not particular about soil but likes a sunny place, and I have put my plants well back in the border, planting them in a close-growing line, and facing them with some shorter and more compact perennial.

To those interested in magic and religion, there is no herb in the garden more worthy of attention, for this simple plant without fragrance, without an outer look of power, without a flower of significance, was singled out from among all other plants and herbs as the most sacred of the growing things of earth between the Pillars of Hercules and the roots of the Caucasus.

Every herb garden should have at least one of the great perennial umbellates. Standing five, six, and even seven feet tall, the smooth and rounded stems of these magnificent herbs soaring together suggest the lesser pillars which enclose the central pillars of many a French thirteenth-century church, and the foliage is the bold gothic foliage of the tympans and the capitals. With Fennel one

can plan a Fennel walk in the English manner,
standing the plants against a comfortable wall,
calling to mind, when the first leaves appear, that
over the leaves of Fennel the women wept for
Thamuz and Adonis. The strong northern biennial
Angelica makes a fine clump, especially when a
little individualized, but of these more anon and
in their place, for the best of the perennial umbellates is to my mind the bold and hardy Lovage.

Not from the slopes of the Mediterranean littoral, but from the mountains and the plateaus
above comes this herb to our gardens, its late Latin
and botanical name *Levisticum* being an uncouth
corruption of Liguria. Rising in the spring from
a very vital and hardy root, it swiftly forms a
clump about a foot high of rounded stalks and
shining dark green leaves with something of the
look and a good deal of the taste of a smooth and
handsome Celery. Its stalks thus placed, its first
leaves opened, the herb rushes from the ground,
the fine hollow columns rising five and six feet
high and taking the leaves with them, the great
umbels of pollen-yellow florets crowning all. Once
used in cookery and domestic medicine, the umbel
fruits are now largely neglected, but the young
shoots, boiled up in a broth, add to it an interesting

LOVAGE

flavor of Celery together with Celery seed. The herb likes a situation in rich soil which retains a proper dampness. Hardy as an oak, vigorous in growth, and interesting to the eye, a clump of Lovage is a fine note among the herbs.

I am often in the garden in the very early morning, for I like the quiet, the heavy dew as yet ungathered from the leaves, the quality of the early light, and the smell of earth soon to be mingled with an occasional clean pungency of smoke from the great kitchen chimney. As the garden begins to gather the eastern light, I often come to think that one of the most beautiful and subtle things in nature is the variation of the color green. There are few things which have a quieter integrity of beauty than the green harmonies of leaves. For some are dark and shining like the Lovage, others pale, each green and each surface making its own byplay with the light; and the greens themselves are rich in variation, ranging from an almost pure blue to yellow. To see both colors upon one plant is a commonplace, for the new growth of blue-green plants is usually a yellow-green. It is by such an economy of means, by such contrasts and transitions that nature varies the entire surface of a world. The silvered darkness of Rue, the fresh green of Basil, and the yellow-green of Costmary are a microcosm of forest and plain, holding the world in a garden as one might hold a leaf in the hollow of a hand.

I once heard from a window on a London street a woman singing the Lavender call. It was not the pretty song so often seen in children's books of music, but another complete and poignant melody, and once and twice and then far-off it rose, touching the heart with its human beauty before it dissolved away into the morning. Something in the soil and climate of southern England, something in the English character, have made Lavender their own, and with it there will always be a thought of its tall spikes against the whitewashed walls of cottages, and of Lavender walks leading from the kitchen garden to the flowers. So cherished indeed is the plant in England, and so many centuries long its garden history, that English Lavender as we know it is the type *Lavandula Vera* no more, but a special and very beautiful garden strain.

English Lavender is one of the really great garden plants. Developed from a Mediterranean form, it grows in English borders to be a handsome shrubby plant two and three feet tall, the leaved shoots rising erect from a contorted main stem and its branches, the leaves narrow and gray-green, the spikes comely and rising somewhat above the plant, the flowers a fine tone of the color to which the herb has given a name. This is the traditional "Sweet Lavender," the plant of the herbalists, the gardeners, and the perfumers, the source of the best and most fragrant essences, the herb whose seeds have been used immemorially for linen closets. In France they plant both a French strain of *L. Vera* and a strain grown from imported English seed, together with the broader leaved but less fragrant Lavender known to them as "Aspic" (*L. Spica*). Some botanists, by the way, classify *L. Vera* as a garden form of *L. Spica*, and as such it is entered in various English catalogues, which is a little confusing. With this nomenclature, however, I do not agree, thinking *L. Vera* more probably a separate species. It is not always an easy plant to find. Practically all nurseries here carry "Lavender," but the buyer will receive about as many different kinds of "Lavender" as there are nurseries. Now it is an English horticultural strain of dwarf Lavender, now a tufted broad-leaved hybrid of some mysterious provenance, now a stout

cutting of *L. Stoechas* grown in America for rock-
eries and mingling its faint aroma of Lavender
with a hearty smell of turpentine, now the actual
L. Vera itself, growing with the crabbed unwil-
lingness it manifests in eastern North America.

Outside of California, where any Lavender
flourishes, the growing of the herb is an uncertain
adventure in American gardens. Every once in a
rare while a gardener finds himself confronted
with a European-minded plant, a plant which
though completely at home in England or in
northern Europe, will hardly grow at all in a not
very dissimilar American northeast, and Lavender
is a typical plant of this kind. *L. Vera* is the best
variety to buy, not only because it is the herb, but
also because it winters as well as any of the species.
Plants which have any chance of flowering should
be trimmed in the autumn and never in the spring.
Disregarding all horticultural practice, I do not
put my plants in a position mercilessly open to our
sun, but in a border situation where they are sheltered by adjoining plants and have their full share
of broken shade. The Lavender I find most satisfactory, I must admit, is not the herb, but the beautiful species known as *L. Dentata*, a fine Lavender
with toothed leaves and tall, symmetrical spikes.

Added to the herbs in June, it thrives with the change, coming into outdoor flower late in August or early in September and making a very charming show. Indeed, it is still in bloom when I have to bring it back into the house, for it is not a hardy plant. *L. Dentata* is rather difficult to find, but it is sometimes carried by dealers in unusual plants.

Herbal Lavender was well known to the Romans, who carried on an almost modern traffic in toilet unguents, bath waters, and perfumes, and they would seem to have used it much as we do, making an extract or decoction of it and adding it to the bath. The word "Lavender" clearly goes back through mediæval Latin to the memory of such a usage, for it is related to the classical Latin verb *lavare* meaning "to wash."

I look about the garden, as I close this introductory group of the greater herbs, and wonder what hints and small counsels I might add to help out another gardener? There's Basil: I buy it from a nursery in flats of a dozen plants apiece, it being a little slow to come from seed, not a plant to be handled roughly, for its root system is small and pulls easily out of the earth; there's Balm: if a bed gets to looking crowded, it is best thinned out in the spring; there's Bergamot Mint: a very easy

plant to propagate, for its creeping stems will strike
root at the nodes when extended along the earth
and pegged down with clothes-pins; there's Rue,
which roots easily from cuttings; and there's Lavender, which is best transplanted in midsummer.

Every once in a while now as I work in the garden in the late afternoon, kneeling by the herbs
and mislaying things and finding them again, some
new small bird, some warbler of the inland country making his way down the lakes to the great
rivers and the sea, catches the corner of my eye as
he moves in the apple branches. A flight of blue-
birds has already passed, though I sometimes still
hear a bluebird's autumnal call, that sweet clear
note with something in it of the plover's tone. The
garden has never looked better than it does this
very afternoon. The plants are all thrifty, the
moisture-loving kinds having taken on a new vig-
or since the rains, and though leaves may be falling, the old apple and pear remain perseveringly
green. The Pot Marjoram is still in flower, the
Thymes keep their own midsummer, and Sweet
Cicely unfolds again a fernlike leaf, the green
of the younger sprays of Balm is as the green of
spring. Surely no plants ever gave so long and lovely a reward. Yet the frosts draw near. Day in the

garden now is almost as quiet as the night, and the dark comes with stars and cold. Working here this afternoon, I think to myself that I have only touched upon the rich treasure of herbs, and must presently come to speak of their larger confraternity.

OF MANY HERBS OF MANY KINDS

CHAPTER III

Of Many Herbs of Many Kinds

It is winter, and the short-lived and silent day has come to an end over the great landscape of snow, closing at sundown with a sky of frozen pink and channels of clearest green; now clouds and the night make together a greater silence and dark; and snow has again begun to fall. Within the house the lamps are lit, each filled to its brim with oil against the long usage of the hours, and the little parlor is comfortable with yellow light and a wood stove's fragrant warmth. It is yellow birch which burns in that sable bastille, yellow birch which kindles so readily and whose bright flames send up from chimneys so unmistakable a smoke. And still it snows, falling through the pitch-black and windless night, feathering over the uneven footing of the shoveled paths, ridging twig and branch anew, and deepening the white levels of the lake.

Where the great Basils stood, and the Lavender was put to have its share of the sun, is now all under a good three feet of snow. No longer the wild, beautiful cries of the loon break at strange hours from the lake, on unsettled, rainy days prophesying still more rain; the crows are with us only when it thaws. Jays, who are not often seen or heard here in the summer, are now the most familiar birds, coming to the doors of barns for seeds of fodder which have been shaken from the lofts down upon the snow, and taking to the fence like sparrows when the farm cats pass. The partridges, too, are foraging. There are lilacs by the shed, and late yesterday afternoon, almost at nightfall, as I chanced to pass the huge, frozen bushes on my way to the spring, six of the birds broke from them in a commotion of winged sound, and vanished as by magic into the last of sunset and the luminous darkness on the fields.

A winter evening is the best of times to muse on plans for a garden, for like Bunyan's *Pilgrim's Progress*, gardening is then carried on "under the similitude of a dream." The things we mean to have stand as we mean to have them, thrifty, beautiful, and a pretty tribute to our skill as gardeners; the things we have had, successes and less-than-successes, are something to go on from, are a part of garden history and our lives. On the table, tumbled over the books, on the floor beside the chair, are an armful of the herb-garden plans, catalogues, letters, left-overs, seed packets, garden notes, and general ambitions, and the aromatic scent of herb seeds is already in the lamplit air. Here in this corner, cut from a yellow envelope and sealed with a fold, is more of the Marjoram which is the Hyssop of Scripture, a green papery seed with a dry, agreeable, and delicately bitter smell—the Hyssop of the lintels of Egypt, and of that tragic draught offered and refused. Here is Coriander, rattling like dry rain in its small box, its seeds like chaffy pills, ancient Coriander of the delta of Egypt, first tasted long ago in a child's cake bought at a shop kept by an elderly Bavarian; here is Dill, fresh and pungent; Burnet which comes so readily from the earth; and the flat Angelica seed which tastes of juniper and bites the tongue. But now to garden musings of the winter kind, and a talk of herbs while the fire blazes and the night is young.

2

The growing of a first few herbs is the discovery of a whole new world of garden pleasure and human meaning, but it is when a gardener has tried a few, liked them and been liked by them and would go on that the full adventure begins. Then it is that a preliminary devil lies in wait to urge the eager soul to put in everything which calls itself an "herb," all in the hope of dragging down the garden of herbs into the curious pit into which gardens have so generally fallen. Avaunt, devil, brother to slugs who work in the night like housebreakers, stealing leaves like spoons, and disappearing somewhere out of the night's window, brother to whatever abominable insect it is which bores a hole in the top of a rose branch, seals it above and below, and inserts an infant worm. No, gardener, put in only the real herbs of the human inheritance and only as many of these as you can care for and come to know and cherish, only as many as you can bind into a living relation to yourself, else you will miss the true quality and unique refreshment of gardening with herbs. Should a genuine rarity come your way, take it when you

can get it, find a place for it and rejoice—that is
understood.

In the following pages I am to discuss a general
list of herbs which seem to me worthy of being
added to the garden or of making their appearance
there from time to time. No authentic gardener
could possibly wish to have them all at once, to
destroy in a seizure of garden greediness all that
the future holds of change and interest. The first
ten herbs recommended were Basil, Marjoram,
Balm, Bergamot Mint, Sage, Hyssop, Rue, Spike
Vervain, Lovage, and Lavender. To increase this
first selection of ten to an ampler two dozen, I
would now add Thyme, Applemint, Dill, Burnet,
Rosemary, Borage, Chives, Costmary, Southernwood, Santolina, Cerinthe, Wormwood (*Artemisia
Absinthium*), Sweet Woodruff, and Valerian.

One has to be a little careful with the THYMES.
Rock gardening brought in the Thymes in force,
and a garden list of them is now so large that it is
just another confusion. In a general sense, any form
of Thyme may be planted as an "herb," but in a
stricter sense the term belongs to a few species with
a long garden history: *Thymus Vulgaris* or Garden
Thyme, which is the true culinary herb; *T. Ser-*

pyllum or Wild Thyme or Shepherd's Thyme, and
T. Herba-Barona or Caraway Thyme. The kitchen
herb is to be had from nurseries in a "broad-leaved"
or "narrow-leaved" strain (the leaves being so
small that it makes not the slightest practical difference), and arrives as a miniature bush about
four or five inches high with stems like wooden
wires and a show of small close-growing leaves.
Garden Thyme is an evergreen in its native south
of Europe, and like many another European evergreen which has to pull itself through an American winter, it can look like nothing at all in the
spring, if it has even survived. Give it plenty of
sun, warm, fussily well-drained soil, and keep the
little plants together. It can be grown quite well
from seed. If the plant grows poorly, one need not
split a hair, but search out some plants of *T. Fra-
grantissimus*, a much stronger little bush and a very
pretty one, or of *T. Citriodorus*, another vigorous
bush with delightfully fragrant leaves and charming heads of bloom. They should be banked for the
winter like miniature roses. *T. Vulgaris*, however,
is the true herb, and an interesting presence to
know and to have.

WILD THYME (*Thymus Serpyllum*) is the little
perennial creeping Thyme which grows every-

where in Europe. There are fields of it on the downs of England, it grows in the gullies of the Channel cliffs, the French Midi is full of it; it was once a part, and perhaps still is, of the ruins and cascades at Tivoli. In France, it is the "Serpolet" of a world of folklore and rustic song; in England, the Thyme of popular legend and Shakespeare's almost too familiar bank. Of this plant famously given to all kinds of variation in form, habit, and color, my garden contents itself with two varieties chosen for their interest and hardiness: Margined Thyme (*T. S. Aureus-Marginatus*), a form with sage-green leaves edged with a line of ivory; and the type *T. Serpyllum* with bright, sun-reflecting leaves. The Margined Thyme grows as a tuft, the type *T. Serpyllum* as a woody creeper. Well-drained earth is essential to these creeping and half-creeping Thymes, all of them natives of dry, limestone soils, and our autumnal rains disturb them. Seeds of the *T. Serpyllum* are to be had without difficulty, but it is much better to buy plants. *T. Herba-Barona*, the old caraway-scented Thyme, is harder to obtain, but a bush or two is worth having. English growers usually carry seed.

A plant of Thyme in flower is a delight in the garden. The woody growth, the tiny leaves and branchlets of leaves, the strong Thyme odor strengthened by the sun—all these make it not a plant to stand and look down at, but to see from its own level and with a thought of its own scale. The Thymes are herbs of the classical world, plants of the old agriculture and the gods, the proverbial bee-pasture of husbandry and poetry, the symbol of things cherished and of honeyed and fragrant sweetness. Where they grow, the shadows which enclose the old classical imagery always seem to lift a little, allowing us to see again the farmhouse with its Roman tiles, the spring clearer than crystal, and Soracte white with snow. The Greeks dried the herb and used it to make a fragrant flame at sacrifices, and from this usage and the Greek verb meaning "to offer sacrifice," it has its name.

APPLEMINT (*Mentha Gentilis*) was one of the favorite herbs of old-time New England, and I often come upon it in old gardens in Maine. It is the smallest and neatest of the household Mints, and like New England architecture at its eighteenth-century best, combines restraint of line with social elegance. It comes in two forms, a type-form with red stems and smooth green leaves, and an old garden form with green stems and leaves variegated in green and golden ivory. My simpler form tends

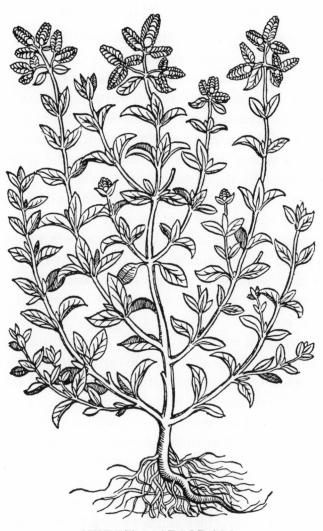

SWEET MARJORAM

to grow as a series of little bushy stalks five and six inches high; the variegated form (which is the stronger, handsomer, and more fragrant) as a little sprawling bush. Both are delightful plants to have, and quite new to all but gardeners with herbs. Stalks of Applemint are perfection for putting into drinks whose delicacy of flavor would be overwhelmed by the stronger Spearmint. The flavor of the herb is the mint flavor with a touch of something unusual added—is it rhubarb? Give Applemint some sun and shade and earth which will not dry out, and take a plant of the Variegated in as a houseplant during the winter. The herb is not entirely easy to obtain, but it is worth the search.

DILL (*Anethum Graveolens*), so familiar as a name and unfamiliar as a living thing, is one of the most beautiful and distinguished plants I think I have ever seen. It is a study in the elements of pure form and the qualities of delicacy and grace, and I always find those who have a living awareness of form in nature curious to know its name. It comes up as a round stem which is at the same time delicate and resolved, and begins to branch simply, the branches being sheathed about the supporting stem, their color blue-green. Above these branches, above the filament leaves fine as the thongs of the symbolic whip of the Egyptian overseer, appear the great double umbels which are five and six inches across when the plant is strong and well grown. The flowers are only dots of an odd yellow at the ends of the umbel stems; it is the umbel itself as a form which is so fine. A quick-growing annual, Dill comes readily from seed. I sow a row or two in a flat, pick out the half-dozen strongest seedlings, and put them in the border where they can have shelter from the full force of the wind.

Dill is in wide and living use. The northern European peoples have a great liking for it, and in Finland, and in Norway and Sweden, it is grown on every farm. Broken up a little, the tender and unripe umbels are excellent in an occasional salad, and the ripe seeds can be kept for the tops of cakes and for making a Dill vinegar. Dill is a plant of the old "witchcraft," of that curious fertility religion which had a separate life of its own during the great ages of the Church and was finally exterminated in the later Renaissance, having become debased. It is a plant of Pan become Lucifer but still keeping his hoofs and horns, a plant of the god who cannot create out of the void but only out of a created world, and who shakes all things with the earthly ecstasy.

BURNET (*Poterium Sanguisorba*) seems little known in America, yet it is a pretty and very usable herb. One of the most vigorous of seedlings, a plant of Burnet grows from a central root, lifting up its pinnate leaves and edged leaflets till it becomes a fountain of green, some four or five inches high. The flowers, which are only a kind of catkin or clover-head, should be kept cut out while the herb is in use. Here Burnet serves as an edging and as a grace of the salad bowl. The leaves have a fresh leafy taste of cucumber and are very pleasant mixed in with the lettuce and a scatter of other herbs. Only the younger leaves should be used and these snipped two or three times across with scissors. Burnet may be grown either as an annual or a perennial and grows best and winters best in properly drained ground. To the French it is *Pimprenelle*, and they sow it in dry fields as a fodder plant, and in kitchen gardens as an herb. It is old. The Romans knew it well, and Lord Bacon wrote in its praise.

ROSEMARY, like Lavender, is another exile in our North and East. The herb of remembrance, symbol of memory as tenderness, of loving thought remaining fragrant and green, it is perhaps not entirely unfitting that it should be an exile on our coasts. So profound and moving, however, are its human associations that a garden of herbs must sometime or other come to have it, doing with it what it can. To my mind the best and most civilized way to have Rosemary in the North is to grow it as a house plant which can in summer be put with the herbs. Plants which are not adapted to the seasonal rhythm of North America have to face in our winter a kind of annual murder, and Rosemary is a defenceless, only quarter-hardy Mediterranean evergreen. As a pot-grown plant there are two ways of treating it. The herb usually arrives from a nursery as a small sprig raised from a cutting, and by trimming this sprig and its shoots with judgment and care, a pot shrub or miniature tree can often be grown. A second treatment consists in letting the wandering side-shoots and top-heavy main stem sprawl as they will till the years grow a great coil of fragrance in the bowl of a pot or jar. Horticulture recognizes this second habit and enters a "prostrate" variety of the plant upon its lists.

The herb flourishes in southern England, and again like Lavender, grows magnificently in California. It needs clean, well-drained soil, sunlight, plenty of air, and a disciplined use of water. A few broken fragments of rock from a limestone country are especially good in the bottom of the pot.

BORAGE (*Borago Officinalis*) I plant simply for its flowers. They are star-shaped, pendent, about an inch across, and of a blue which is surely one of the most beautiful in nature. In the whiter, paler heart of each blue star is a massed cone, not of black but of blackish-brown anthers, a color adjacence of much more interest and subtlety. Such a blue in the ancient magic of colors and symbols was always the color of the mind as a force: in blue was the divine mind itself reflected. The plant as a whole is vigorous and bristly, its lower leaves being of no value, but the top leaves are sometimes put into drinks to add a doubtful flavor of cucumber. Borage is a plant of honorable antiquity, having been mentioned by Pliny and recommended as a cup-bearer of courage and good cheer.

The herb is a quick-growing annual of the easiest culture, attaining a height of about fourteen inches. I sow the seed in a flat, choose my best ten or a dozen seedlings, and put them in the border as a group, a show of Borage in flower being a delightful sight. When not in the herb garden, Borage is an excellent plant to grow beside the peas and beans. Flowers in a vegetable garden humanize it and make it more pleasant to be in and work in. That original combination of morning glories and scarlet-runner beans beloved of the French farmer should be cheerful under our American sky.

CHIVES go in for both gardener and cook. As a decorative plant they have never had their due here, though the Europeans make a great deal of them and catalogue a number of varieties. The large cylindrical stalks, the flower heads like flattened spheres stuck with tufts of lilac, make a bold and interesting show in the later spring. Garden Chives (*Allium Schoenoprasum var. Sibericum*) belong with onions and garlic bulbs to the lily family, and the original plant from which the garden variety is descended grows wild in North America and Eurasia. Give a mat of chives a share of both sun and shade, earth which will not dry out round the fine roots, and cut the flower stalks off close to the ground the moment they are through flowering. Chives are among the hardiest of perennial herbs.

COSTMARY is called "Sweet Tongue," here in Maine, and grows half wild on the edges of old orchards and near old farms. It is a simple and rather rustic herb, *"de plus rustique,"* as the French catalogues say of country things, but I have a particular liking for it: it has character. A perennial and of the hardiest sort, the herb spreads from a running root, raising itself up as a stalk or group of stalks thickly clothed with whitened oblong leaves which decrease in size as they ascend the stem. Such flowers as it has are but abortive greenish buttons; the quality of the plant is in the mellow old-fashioned fragrance of its leaves.

Costmary is a pleasant herb. A stalk of it reinforces and accentuates the other herbal fragrances in a clutch of herbs, and the leaves make a slightly bitter medicinal tea. Originally an herb of western Asia, it was probably introduced into Europe by way of Greece, for Greek physicians were intelligently interested in the medicinal qualities of plants. Indeed, the very English-sounding name is of Greek derivation, and freely translated means Balm of (St.) Mary. In Botany the plant bears the impressive designation *Chrysanthemum Balsamita var. Tanacetoides.*

SOUTHERNWOOD (*Artemisia Abrotanum*), long a border plant as well as an herb, is still called "Lad's Love" in old-fashioned gardens. It is really

BERGAMOT MINT

a small perennial shrub which puts forth a certain amount of tender aromatic growth every year, some of which is lost during the winter and some retained. The leaves, like those of Dill, are filaments of green. I have just one bush which stands in sun and broken shade and out of reach of the wind. The fragrance seems to vary in quality with individual plants, some having the strong but pleasant herb-and-turpentine smell which the French declare is sovereign against moths, others almost no scent at all. The name "Lad's Love," which has been explained in so many pretty and fanciful ways, is an exact translation of the name of the plant in classic Greek. Nurseries often have Southernwood or can get it. Said by botanists to be a native of Continental Europe, it is probably an herb of temperate Asia as well, for I am told that it is well-known in Chinese gardens. Southernwood is a quiet, pleasant, civil thing in a garden, a fit neighbor for Chinese philosophers discussing life and poetry by a pool.

SANTOLINA, for some absurd reason now called "Lavender Cotton," was called "Ground Cypress" by the Romans, a title lately usurped by Kochia, that perfect plant for the entrance to one's garage. It is a pity that the classical name has thus been filched, for it is much the best of the herb's various names, and belongs to it by an honorable inheritance of over two thousand years. What the herb really suggests more than anything else is a little tree a foot high of silvery green-gray coral. It has no leaves in any familiar sense of the word. Once used by the Romans as a medicinal herb and discussed by Pliny, Santolina is now entirely a decorative plant. A little bush here and there makes an interesting study in form and color, and the coral-like growth has an aromatic fragrance rather like a milder Tansy. Some use it as an edging, but I think it perhaps too sharply individualized and conspicuous for such a use, except in a very formal way. The herb makes no particular demands, asking simply to be put in a warm and well-drained soil and let alone to thrive, establish itself, and bear its catkin flowers. My plants make cypress-shaped bushes about a foot high, and I have put them where they are not swung about by the wind. For a Mediterranean evergreen, Santolina winters unexpectedly well—only be sure to watch for it in the spring, give it care, and help to get it going.

CERINTHE or Honeywort will be a new plant, I imagine, to most growers of herbs. It is the pretty yellow-flowered bee herb of Virgil and the Latin historians of agriculture; eighteenth-century editions of the Georgics often have a figure of it, the old ink turned brown upon the brown and ivory plate. Pliny describes it, and to quote from the notes in an old Virgil, "Philagyrius says it derives its name from a city of Boetia where it grows in great plenty." Philagyrius I know not, but Cerinthe grows well for me, becoming a strong, rather rustic plant, and its small, bell-shaped yellow flowers and spotted, alternate leaves are a pleasant feature in a garden whose flowers are so many of them in tones of violet and purple. The seed of the herb must be purchased abroad. Two kinds are usually available, *Cerinthe Alpina* from northern Italy and the Tyrol, and *C. Retorta* from Greece, both perennials. The plants are considered hardy, but I have not had them long enough to vouch for that side. A vigorous herb, Cerinthe needs room, good garden soil, and its share of sun. Good plants grow to be about twelve and fourteen inches high.

WORMWOOD is all at once a drug, a symbol, and an herb. A tonic dose of bitters has always had a certain medical value, and "Wormwood" was the bitter of the ancients, being distilled from the leaves of various bitter Artemisias, and especially from the plant *Artemisia Absinthium*. Known to the peoples of the Roman Empire and in wide use, particularly esteemed in the Middle Ages, *A. Absinthium* retained its medical reputation well into the later seventeenth century, and then began to lose it, the plant itself retreating during its eclipse from the gardens of great houses to cottage gardens, and from cottage gardens to the roads. It is now, however, widely grown again, this time as the source of the active ingredient of absinthe and various other bitter liqueurs, "Wormwood" and "Vermouth" being forms of the same word. As a symbol, Wormwood stood for what was bitter and troubling to the soul. One thinks of Hamlet's sullen mumble of "Wormwood, wormwood," as he listens to the player queen's protestations, and of that furious star named Wormwood which fell from heaven across the darkened sky of the Book of Revelation and made bitter one third of the waters of the earth. *A. Absinthium* can with patience be grown from seed, but it is better to get plants which are once again being offered by the nurseries. The herb is gray-green in color, and the much-divided leaves are silky on both sides; it grows to be two or three feet high and becomes shrubbier as it thrives. I find it a reliably hardy perennial. Slugs have a horrible absinthe craving for its leaves, and unless held off will eat them to the bone. Another Wormwood, Roman Wormwood (*A. Pontica*), is often seen in old gardens of herbs, a vigorous, spreading, gray-green affair which should have a corner all its own. The culinary herb Tarragon (*A. Dracunculus*) is the only one of the Artemisias with *simple* leaves. In buying plants beware of any with divided leaves, for these are the "false tarragon" which dealers frequently offer for the true. A plain, branching plant, it is not much to look at as an herb, but those who like its flavor can easily find a place for it as a bit of green. It is a tender perennial which does not produce seed in the North, and is propagated by cuttings.

SWEET WOODRUFF (*Asperula Odorata*) is an herb for a shady corner, especially a corner it can have for its own. It is a neat and pretty plant, standing six or seven inches high, the foliage fresh and green, the florets snow white, the leaves arranged in a whorl about the stems. It has always been particularly cherished and valued in Germany. Bunches of Woodruff hung up to dry will fill a whole attic with a fragrance like new-mown hay, and dried and seasoned will make an interesting brew often used by Gipsies as a tea. It is a native European plant and a reliable perennial.

VALERIAN is a garden term which covers the virtues of two different plants. The true Valerian of medicine and the older herbalists is *Valeriana Officinalis*, the tall, strong-growing plant with pinnate leaves, high flower stalks, and flat, whitish-lilac flower heads seen so often here in Maine, where it is called "Garden Heliotrope." *V. Officinalis* is one of the hardiest and most dependable of perennials, but it is a rank spreader, and perhaps just a little coarse, so I do not recommend putting it among the herbs. It is an excellent plant, however, for use in the left-overs of space one occasionally encounters on the frontiers of garden areas, and for establishing in half wild situations. I use it on the side of a path leading into the herbs from the North, and there it walls off the wild growth, spreads to its heart's content, and looks very well.

The other Valerian which is also planted as an herb is Red Spur Valerian or "Pretty Betsy" (*Centranthus Ruber*). This herb belongs to the same Valerian tribe as *V. Officinalis* but is quite another sort of thing, being really a pretty, old-fashioned garden plant with flower clusters of an unusual pinkish red. It is a hardy perennial which will do well in almost any garden soil, but responds grate-fully to encouragement, growing about a foot and a half high and continuing in blossom from middle summer into fall. The Valerians are plants of a famous family. The Spikenard of Scripture and the classical authors is a plant of this order, *Nardostachys Jatamansi*. An herb of Butan in India, it was carried by way of Arabia to Asia Minor and thence to the great trade routes of Rome. Valerian is a plant of the old folklore, a protector of house and household from "things which go bump in the night," and children who were afraid to go to bed in the dark were given a sprig of it to put beneath their pillows.

3

So there you have a gardener's first two dozen herbs, chosen and written down on an evening of winter quiet, books, and garden thoughts. The night is still young, shall I run through what is left of my list, saying but a word or two about each herb? A list it will have to be, there's no avoiding it, but I trust it will not seem just another cata-logue of herbs, for it is essentially a personal selec-tion of plants which I have found beautiful, worth knowing, and last but not least, reasonably available. It is folly to plant vegetables, umbellate "greens," garden commonplaces, and herbal duplicates and triplicates when there are all kinds of beautiful and historic things within reach of our hands. Only one of the really great herbs is "lost," the beautiful Dittany I have already mentioned, and for that reason I have not entered it on my working list, nor have I listed the Biblical Hyssop (*Origanum Maru*) or the Mandrake (*Mandragora Officinarum*), both gifts, and as far as I know not to be had from any American or European house. The list to follow includes, I think, the body of any table of herbs, together with a few which have not yet been discussed. But to the list, perennials it shall be, and no favorites this time but *a* and *b* by the alphabet.

1. AGRIMONY (*Agrimonia Eupatoria*), an old-fashioned country herb with a mediæval reputation as a panacea; flowers yellow and in tapering spikes; whole plant faintly aromatic; grows one to two feet high; makes an herb tea. Seeds may be had from French seedsmen. Botanically related to American Agrimony (*A. Hirsuta*). A homespun, simple plant, but a tuft or two of it interesting, best put in a not too conspicuous place. Cut the flowers after blooming.

2. ALTHEA (*Althea Officinalis*), the country "Marsh-Mallow" of old-fashioned medicine, grows about two feet high, has soft, downy leaves and axillary branchlets of small rosy purple or bluish purple flowers of the Hollyhock kind. A very old herb, useful for flower color, easy to raise, not to be confused with *Malva Moschata*. Best seeds from France.

3. ANGELICA (*Angelica Officinalis*), a tall, very hardy biennial growing four to six feet high with a huge umbellate flower and leaves very like celery leaves. Difficult to grow from seed; when trying, get only the very freshest autumnal seed and sow outside a day or two before the ground freezes. Inside sowing of fall seed not recommended to those who have no greenhouse. An herb worth having; nurseries ought to carry it.

4. BAYBERRY (*Myrica Carolinensis*), a native plant so familiar that it is rarely seen with awareness. Well worth having to represent the sweet shrubs. Leaves have a fragrance resembling that of the true Bay with which it was once confused. Bayleaf of cookery comes from a true Laurel (*Laurus Nobilis*); our Bayberry is a Myrtle, and its virtues are esthetic and medical.

5. BEE BALM (*Monarda Didyma*), called "Ber-

HYSSOP

gamot" by the English, a native American long naturalized in gardens. Comes in tones of scarlet, magenta and even pinkish-white; get plants of the older strains, as their leaves are better proportioned to the blossom than are the leaves of the newer hybrids; beware rusts.

6. CAMOMILE (*Anthemis Nobilis*), an humble tuft of pretty fern-like greenery; mildly aromatic; dried flowers make a famous tisane; good for rockwork and a relief from Sedums.

7. CAMPHOR BALSAM (*Balsamita Vulgaris*), an old-fashioned rustic plant with green-gray leaves smelling of camphor; grows from twelve to eighteen inches high; an interesting garden companion to Costmary. Seeds to be had from English growers.

8. CLARY or "CLEAR-EYES" (*Salvia Sclarea*), a fine biennial sage growing about two feet high; leaves woolly; flowers borne on a spike and cupped with contrasting bracts. Will flower first year, if started early; keep basal leaves protected from slugs. Seeds from England or France. A decoction of the mucilaginous seeds of this plant was used as an eyewash.

9. COMFREY (*Symphytum Officinale*), a large rough plant with a liking for moisture; flowers

are interestingly placed. Called "Comforty Root"
in New England. Has a long history in popular
medicine. Very hardy and well worth having. Not
in cultivation, but often found in old gardens.

10. ELECAMPANE (*Inula Helenium*), not in
scale with the rest of the herbs, and best put by
itself. Resembles a Brobdingnagian Dock with
ragged composite flowers; very hardy, and sometimes seen growing as a weed. Elecampane or
"Horse-Heal" is the historic herb of the horse-
loving peoples coming with them out of Central
Asia and going with them and the horse to the
ends of the earth. Can be had from dealers in native
plants.

11. FENNEL or PERENNIAL FENNEL (*Foeni-
culum Officinale*), another tall herb of the umbellate type with bright yellow florets and feathery
leaves; comes easily from seed; much resembles
Dill. Worth trying when the garden is ready for
change and variety among its umbellate herbs.
Leaves used in salads and as an hors d'œuvre; also
as a flavoring in sauces.

12. FUMITORY (*Fumaria Officinalis*), another
rustic European herb of country medicine and folklore, botanically related to the familiar "Bleeding
Heart"; flowers rose tipped with purple; height

about twelve to eighteen inches, a quiet, inconspicuous, rather interesting plant whose smoke,
"*fumus*," was once thought to have the power of
expelling demons. Seeds to be had from France.

13. GERMANDER (*Teucrium Chamaedrys*), well
called by the French "Little Oak" from its manner of growth and the shape of its leaves; none too
hardy; pretty as a specimen plant or a pot plant,
and a distinguished edging where the climate
permits.

14. GOAT'S RUE (*Galega Officinalis*), a very
ancient plant which has served both as an agricultural plant and as an herb. Has pretty showy clusters of purplish blue Sweet-Pea-shaped flowers;
hybrids now available; grows bushily between two
and three feet tall. Seeds to be had from either
French or English seedsmen.

15. MONK'S HERB (*Mentha Rotundifolia*), a
large, vigorous, sprawly mint with thick stalks
and large woolly leaves; smells like Spearmint
with a ranker overtone. Was much used in monas-
tic medicine; makes a very fair tisane, as the ob-
jectionable flavor does not carry over. Sometimes
called "Woolly Mint." Beware leaf-eating insects
and caterpillars. Plants may be had from American nurseries.

16. PENNYROYAL, English kind (*Mentha Pulegium*), stems prostrate and creeping, leaves small and oval, a vigorous ground runner, taking root as it spreads; likes a damp situation. Odor resembles that of American Pennyroyal, but is heavier and more medicinal. Makes a tea famous as a remedy for colds. Not really hardy; can be used as a house herb.

17. PEPPERMINT (*Mentha Piperita*), a vigorous hardy Mint of a bushy and rather sprawly habit, but with neat leaf branches and neat leaves. Can be used as an occasional substitute for Spearmint in cold drinks, and dried for an excellent winter tea. Peppermint of commerce distilled from this plant. A few clumps are worth having.

18. PULMONARIA (*Pulmonaria Officinalis*), or Lungwort, a close relative of our *Mertensia Virginica* and sometimes called "Soldiers and Sailors" from the same two-color effect of the flowers, has leaves interestingly spotted with white. Was used for maladies of the chest. Various Pulmonarias are offered by French and English seedsmen; *Pulmonaria Officinalis* a little difficult to obtain.

19. SAFFRON (*Crocus Sativus*), an autumn Crocus with a long history as a drug, a flavoring powder, and a pigment, only the golden stigmata of

the flower being used. Pretty but capricious as a
garden plant, often refusing to flower. Needs winter protection.

20. SPEARMINT (*Mentha Viridis*), probably
the most familiar of the perennial herbs. Will
grow almost anywhere but has best flavor in the
shade; new and tenderer growth can be brought
out by frequent cutting. Of this plant the French
make their best *infusion de menthe*.

21. SWEET CICELY (*Myrrhis Odorata*), an old
herb of the umbellate family with an aromatic
and very beautifully divided leaf. Grows to be
about two feet tall from a fern-like clump. Difficult to raise from seed. Use same procedure recommended for Angelica. Seeds to be had from
England or France. If unsuccessful in raising it,
try its close relative, "American Sweet Cicely"
(*Osmorhiza Longistylis*), a smaller native plant
with the same delicacy of leaf. Can be obtained
from dealers in native plants, and is well worth
having whether or not you have *Myrrhis Odorata*.

22. SWEET MAUDLIN (*Achillea Ageratum*), another very old-fashioned cottage plant; has yellow
flowers and an aromatic fragrance; grows about
two feet high and comes easily from seed; makes a
third with Costmary and Camphor Balsam.

23. WINTER SAVORY (*Satureia Montana*), a shrubby herb more attractive as a little plant than as a large one; fairly hardy; said to make an attractive edging where climate permits.

24. WOAD (*Isatis Tinctoria*), an interesting European plant closely related to our familiar weed the wild Radish; a little coarse in growth; has yellow flowerets on stalks. Famous as the herb with which the ancient Britons used to dye themselves blue. The French call it "*Pastel*" and sell it as a forage plant.

25. WOUNDWORT (*Stachys Betonica* or *S. B. Officinalis*), a rugged clump of heart-shaped leathery leaves on leathery stems; "heads" of rose-purple flowers similar to the flower heads of the common Prunella or "Self Heal"; very hardy; needs broken shade and moisture in the ground. Offered by various American nurseries. Not a plant for the front of the border, but a good one for shady corners under large plants.

4

The handful of herbs remaining (with the exception of Caraway, which is a biennial) are annuals or plants usually treated as annuals. All are of interest, and three or four are especially worth a trial. A group of umbellates with aromatic "seeds" or fruits, Anise and Cumin, Caraway, and Coriander begin the list.

1 & 2. ANISE and CUMIN (*Pimpinella Anisum* and *Cuminum Cyminum*), two very old herbs from the warmer countries of the eastern Mediterranean, Cumin with rose-colored florets being the more interesting but the more difficult to grow. Sow them both where they are to stand and in a warm position, for both are bad transplanters and need heat. One's luck with Cumin in the North depends a good deal on the kind of summer, but it should do particularly well in the South. Anise grows to be about fourteen inches high, Cumin to about ten or twelve inches. Both are used in the manufacture of cordials and liqueurs. These herbs are interesting for their Biblical and classical background, but are of no great distinction as plants.

3. CARAWAY (*Carum Carvi*), one of the commonest of field herbs here in Maine, having been brought into the state by the Waldoboro Germans in the eighteenth century. Those who have not seen it and chance to like the fresh Caraway flavor will find it quick to come from seed, useful, and more of a farm-garden plant than an herb. It much resembles a minor "Queen Anne's Lace."

SPIKE VERVAIN

4. CORIANDER (*Coriandrum Sativium*), the best, to my mind, of these four seed-bearing herbs. It is much the strongest and hardiest, comes without difficulty, if a little slowly, from seed, and the "seeds" or fruits, once dried and rid of their green rankness, can always be used in spice candies and pastries. If given a good start, Coriander grows to be about two feet high; in sowing it, it is well to face the row due south. When the Israelites murmured for the fleshpots of Egypt and the fish "which we did eat in Egypt freely," they added that the manna which bored them had a taste of Coriander seed. As these four herbs die down rather quickly, it is best not to grow them near the longer lived perennials or where a "gone" spot in the garden will be conspicuous.

5. CHERVIL (*Anthriscus Cerefolium*), a pretty, fine-leaved herb used in salads. It makes a ferny bed of greenery and tastes pleasantly of Parsley mingled with Caraway. It is easy to grow and worth trying.

6. POT MARIGOLD (*Calendula Officinalis*), merely our Calendula in its small, single, and old-fashioned form, and as such is pretty in a garden of herbs, the great double modern Calendulas hav-

ing no place there. The best seeds are to be had from England.

7. HOLY THISTLE (*Carduus Benedictus*), a handsome annual from southern Europe once considered a sovereign restorative and still having some reputation, but turn to *Much Ado About Nothing*, Act III, Scene IV, where the ladies Beatrice and Hero discuss Margaret's saying, "Get you some of this distilled Carduus Benedictus, and lay it to your heart; it is the only thing for a qualm." Carduus is easy to raise, and well worth trying some year as a decorative plant. Seeds of it are still to be found in the flower section of the French catalogues.

8. JOB'S TEARS (*Coix Lacrimae Jobi*), a grass discovered in the East Indies during the seventeenth century and with the good imaginative vigor of the past promptly distributed over Europe as a cure-all. Strung on a strong thread, the oddly shaped, pendent seed cases are still sold in pharmacies as an aid to infant teething. The plant comes easily from seed and grows to be anywhere from twelve to twenty-four inches. Well worth more attention from herbalists, as it is picturesque in itself and can be planted as a representative of

herbal grasses. The seed is to be had from American firms.

9. PARSLEY (*Garum Petroselinum*), today essentially a plant of the *jardin potager*, but in ancient usage and literature an "herb," and as an herb completely worthy of attention and garden use. Sprigs of parsley are so often seen upon a dish and it has so chaste a union with cold meat, that nobody ever looks at it as a plant or sees that it has beauty as well as function. Yet the Greeks made wreaths of it and decorative garlands, dedicating it as a plant to the gods. I use it here (as it is said to have been used in Greece) as an edging, shearing it and cutting it back at need, and finding it very beautiful in color and luxuriance of growth, and very living. Parsley is best bought already started in a flat, as it is slow to come from seed.

10. SUMMER SAVORY (*Satureia Hortensis*), one of the pleasantest of the sweet-herbs, and sooner or later to be tried by every gardener. It grows as a little erect bush about a foot high, and flowers on slender stalks from the axils, the flowerets being a pale lilac in color. Sow this Savory early, getting it started indoors if possible, and leaving about five inches between the seedlings set out. The entire plant is of an agreeable aromatic fragrance and

may be used in the house and the kitchen in a dozen different ways. It is this pleasant annual which is the true *Satureia*, the plant loved of the Satyrs and grown by them in rustic pots on the window ledges of their shelters in the fields. To these leaves and this fragrance they returned from their flocks and vines, their hoofs drumming upon the sunbaked Italian earth, these little branches refreshed for them the oil and the wine. For the Satyr was once a companion to man and a sharer of the earth, hearing the sudden flutter of leaves by the door and knowing the smell of twig wood burning, a great prophet heard him cry to his fellow, and long afterwards a father of the church had with such a one an urbane and distinguished colloquy. This herb is his, coming to us out of the Golden Age, and the seed we sow is a little put between our fingers by those half-human and immortal hands.

5

So closes the garden list, but certain very familiar herbs were not planted in gardens, but only domesticated in and about the old farms. No housewife ever planted Catnip with the Applemint and Balm, it was sown as a "patch" somewhere—"this side of the henhouse" or "down by the shed" and there left to the cats and its own devices. How often one comes upon such patches still, suddenly made aware of the limp, flannel-like leaves of Catnip underfoot by the strong, accusing odor in the air. The same thing was done with the other common herbs of country medicine, the old white Horehound of England (*Marubium Vulgare*), that wan nettle-like presence with its pointed, hostile bracts. It is in such patches that these time-honored but weedy herbs still belong; the garden is not theirs. Both are perennials, though the Catnip plants I oftenest see are the vigorous seedlings which might be annuals and are great travellers; the Horehound as I remember it holds more closely to its place. To this day, patches of Horehound stand back of many old houses on Cape Cod; I often used to come upon them in the Eastham years.

The old-fashioned country pharmacopœia was a quite comprehensive affair. Its materials included Indian recipes of powdered roots and powdered leaves, naturalized European herbs and weeds, and a whole countryside of native herbs and simples which each household gathered after the crops were in, the secret of their growing places being a sort of family inheritance. Sweet Fern and Wild

Ginger, Sassafras and Mullen, Tansy and Colts-
foot, each had its rôle and reputation, and pedlars
from the uplands tramped all New England with
heavy bundles of the prepared leaves swinging
from their shoulders on a yoke. As medicines
(when they were not simply harmless and com-
forting drinks) the infusions were for the most
part either mild stimulants or astringents, oftenest
the latter. Now and then a "simple" was a power-
ful drug, such as Digitalis, which came into medicine from an English "wise woman's" garden, but
these were rare. Here in New England, Catnip
(*Nepeta Cataria*), Thoroughwort (*Eupatoria Per-
foliatum*), Pennyroyal (*Hedeoma Pulegioides*), and
Horehound were the household favorites among
the herbs hanging head downward from the drying
racks in the attic; they are favorites to this day.
Many a boy has choked over a horrible dose of
Thoroughwort about as efficacious as a rabbit's
foot, but Catnip Tea was and is a restorative brew
to drink when weary, and Horehound and Pennyroyal are still valiant against a cold.

A "patch" garden of the old simples might be
a picturesque affair. There one could put the interesting things which have no place with the
great herbs and really prefer a free existence.

American Pennyroyal belongs here, a plant of the pond shores which does not take overkindly to cultivation, though seeds of it are now on sale; Catnip and Horehound; the Calamints or Wild Basils (*Calamintha Clinopodium* and *C. Nepeta*), wild things both, having practically gone out of use; Wild Ginger (*Asarum Canadense*), an interesting perennial; Wintergreen (*Gaultheria Procumbens*) which the English have imported for the beauty of its leaves; Gold Thread (*Coptis Trifolia*)—these last three sold by dealers in native plants. Here Tansy can go in, if you want so familiar a weed at all; the native Wild Mint (*Mentha Canadensis*) with its queerish stick-of-gum smell; the beautiful but more tender Maryland Dittany (*Cunila Origanoides*); Motherwort (*Leonurus Cardiaca*), a picturesque weed once used in popular medicine; and Sweet Flag (*Acorus Calamus*); not cultivated things by any means, nor yet ferally wild, but all touched somehow or other by the hand or the thought of man. A fancy for including really wild simples will lead one across Gray's Botany. To my mind the three most interesting plants of this rather misty group are Wild Ginger, the Wild Mint, and Sweet Flag. I have them here and find them all hardy, and the solitary flower of the Ginger is one of the quaint reassurances of spring.

But it grows late, half the household is already abed, the clock pipes its cheerful cuckoo call over a faint whirr of weights descending, the hour is at hand to give the house over to darkness and the winter night. Now shall the billet of oak be thrust into the stove, all night long to feed a little glow of gnawing flame and keep the core of the house human and warm, the lamps turned down and quenched, the doors secured, and the last hand light carried through the darkened rooms past the silent and familiar things. It has stopped snowing. The north has cleared, and beyond the window of a passage the pole burns blue and cold, touching with the light of stars and space the garden in its drifts and the snow pressed like a wave against the wall. And so to bed, taking with me to their cupboard under the stair the lists, the letters, and the seeds, hearing in their dry rustle and slide the promise of a garden.

OF PLANTING AND GARDENING

CHAPTER IV

Of Planting and Gardening

ANY ACCOUNT OF HERBS would be incomplete if it had nothing to say of the making and planting of a garden. The matter of soil is immemorially the first thing to consider, and with "good garden soil" one is ready to begin. The phrase is politely vague, but no gardener needs of it an elaborate definition, and I take it to mean a soil with a reasonably deep and workable loam, an undersoil favorable to drainage, and that innate vitality which can never be caught in the symbols of chemistry or the frame of an explanation. No soil under heaven will suit everything unless it be that loam we vicariously left behind in the first of gardens: we have to do our best with what we find, and the vast generality of herbs are not crotchety. Plants with a long history and a wide distribution at the hands of man are not of an exacting nature, and make the best of it, like seasoned travellers.

But there are plenty of books and pamphlets concerned with the making of borders and beds, plenty of leaflets about composts and manures and other hearty matters, and I do not intend to go into this elementary side of garden-making. Gardeners worth their salt, moreover, will all have their own pet beliefs, hopes, methods, and materials. There is one hint worth passing on to those who might occasionally prepare a border in the grand manner, which is that a virtue resides in the eighteenth-century practice of putting at the bottom of a well-dug trench a couch of branched saplings or open brush before the enriched earth is replaced. Where the lower soil is heavy and clinging, this antique usage makes for better drainage, and permits deep roots to find their way into the ground. With ordinary "good garden soil" a proper cleaning-up in the fall and a top dressing of old manure is sufficient, though it is also a good plan to rake in some hardwood ashes and a light couch of old dressing in the spring. Too rich a soil breeds watery stems, susceptibility to molds and rankness of growth at the expense of flowers in many plants, though some

will gorge and thrive on it, whilst others ungrate-
fully sicken and stand still.

If the herbs are going to be arranged in a border,
and the garden can manage it, it is well to have
two beds, one with a direct southern exposure, one
with an exposure due east or a little south of east.
This is what I have here and find most successful.
In dealing with plants from other countries, agriculture and gardening do not make enough of a
study of the quality of the light or the nature of
the effects of the American sun. Our sun is a fierce
and barbaric force, an Aztec presence, and the relation to it of the sun of Europe is the relation of a
drawing of Zeus by Flaxman to a mythological
figure chiselled upon a pillar at Copan. Many European plants, even those from the south of Europe
and the Mediterranean, often have a quelled look
in American borders, especially those planted
against a western or southwestern wall. The blaze
is too much for the shorn lamb, and what such
plants need is not so much "shade" as fewer hours
of our intenser light. It is for this reason that I like
borders with various exposures; they enable one to
give plants the amount of our sun they need and
can use. Though I have various plants (not herbs)
growing in the full weight of a summer afternoon

(there are seasoned native plants and tropical up-
land plants well suited to it) I like the herbs to be
in complete shade by the latter part of the afternoon, for by then they have had enough of sun. Under this regimen my herbs flourish. The Thymes
get most sun, but I do not give Lavender the entire
day of it, much to its profit. In a garden in the
open, plants simply have to go through with it,
which they do well enough.

Quite apart from the matter of the duration of
direct light, certain plants prefer that the light
they are given should be tempered, and these I
have indicated by the use of the words "broken
shade." In giving our plants "shade" we rely too
much, I think, on the full blanketing shadows of
walls or close-growing trees, and not enough on
the shade developed within the border itself. A
blanket of shade, like the sun turning the corner of
a house in full force can come down on a plant like
the wolf on the fold. Sometimes the solid shadow
of a wall is inevitable and very necessary, but
more often the broken and living shade of leaves
in movement above them is a better kind of thing.
I try to do this here, putting plants which are
not genuine sun-haters in the shade and shelter of
taller things. The practice is experimental and

needs garden judgment, but the results are good.

To write at length about the watering of plants would again seem to me a folly, for any garden is the child of weather and a thousand circumstances, and only garden judgment can tell a gardener when and how much to use. To water late at night, indeed just before putting the house to bed, is a counsel of perfection, but it is the best thing one can do for a small garden during a spell of great heat and drying-out of the soil. Seedlings and cherished plants establishing themselves should be watered with rain water from a rain barrel kept for that purpose, warmish rain water being an *elixir vitae* to plants. If gardeners will forget a little the phrase "watering the plants" and think of watering as a matter of "watering the earth" under the plants, keeping up its moisture content and gauging its need, the garden will get on very well. It is all tentative; there are times when a garden needs water every night and needs it badly, there are times when an occasional deep soaking is all that it requires. We do not mulch things enough in America during the crest of our hot weather. Another point to be remembered is that one is working with at least two separate types of plants, a Mediterranean group which needs water in moderate quantities and a group of Mints which like a conventional dousing. Do not, however, actually stint the Mediterranean plants of their water, for in spite of their reputation they are not natives of a "dry" region, and it has been my experience that they do not thrive in our Northeast in dry and sun-baked situations. They do well in England in a conventional border, and a like situation is the best place for them here.

Shade-appreciating Mints, sun-loving Thymes, each to its place, and may the garden thrive! The Mints need not be plunged in Stygian shade. They like their share of sun and thrive and blossom the better for it, particularly Peppermint and Apple-mint. The east border is the place for them, with its fewer hours of direct sun; if they have to stand in a south border, then it is well to temper the light received. Entirely apart from the matter of light and shade, two of the mint species, Spearmint and Monk's Herb, should never be put in the actual border, for they are merciless spreaders and grasp-ing colonizers. All other mints can be held in check, even Bee-Balm, whose newer hybrid forms are appallingly vigorous. If there is room for it, it is always well to have an extension garden of herbs in which one can root cuttings, put thriving divisions, and test new varieties and seeds. New plants of shade-appreciating things should have almost complete shade till they are established, and sun-loving things only a ration of the light which they can later sustain.

2

The annuals used in the border should always be selected and featured plants. Sow the seed carefully, being willing to have patience and take time, spacing the larger seeds by hand and avoiding a smother of the smaller kinds. When they come up and are safe to handle, choose the strong seedlings and put aside once and a half the number of plants you intend to use. If your seeds are in a flat, cover it with glass and wipe off the moisture once a day till the plants are seen, then leave off the cover. And get them into the border as soon as it seems safe, and protect them awhile from slugs and other devourers of leaves near the ground. Perennial seeds take longer to appear, and many are best started early in the house so that the plants may be adequately well grown before the frosts. Seeds and seedlings like warmish rain water, and transplanting is best done after sundown. If you wish to give some cherished plant every chance, move it at night—after having prepared the transfer by day. In making a transfer, I first dig a hole for the plant, put in a little rotten manure and loam at the bottom, pepper and salt the sides of the well with a little commercial fertilizer, flood the pit with water, go away and read a book, and then put in the herb with its ball of soil and fill it all in with dry earth, avoiding mud at all costs. The plant is then watered lightly an hour or two later. If herbs arrive potbound from a nursery, wash out the roots in a pail of water, keeping about one fourth of the soil in place, and then plant, opening up the roots as you put them in. Potbound plants have a kind of potbound complex and have to be forced out of it, else they come to nothing.

Because herbs are plants whose outer appeal is one of beauty and distinction of form, gardeners should try to have as good plants as they can and keep the whole garden ordered and thrifty. I always like to have the herbs, especially the taller ones, reasonably sheltered from the wind. When plants are thrashed about and bullied overmuch, the delicate feeding roots and hairs are apt to be broken or injured by the strain on the entire root system, and the plant as it stands above the ground acquires a blowzy look. Insect enemies are not difficult to deal with, having no special liking for herbs, and I have to do very little spraying. Only once in a garden while will a pest visit an herb and have to be cleaned off or a caterpillar solitary begin to riddle the leaves of Balm and Bergamot Mint. Monk's Herb is their favorite victim. Aphises are practically unknown, and if any herb of the selections should chance to attract them, take it out. The pests will come, however, if the gardener adds to the herb garden various associate garden plants which are not herbs, the Rose Geranium, for instance, in which the green aphis is completely and detestably at home. Slugs have a liking for absinthe, but of that I have spoken; in hunting for them at night, it is well to look around the edges of their canebrake, the Chives. And now a counsel to be spoken with the tongues of men and angels: if you have to spray anything in the herb garden, always spray with something non-poisonous to human beings. Never, never, never use a poisonous spray anywhere near these plants of domestic and human use.

There should always be flower color in a garden of herbs, but no conspicuously flowering herb or group of such herbs should ever be suffered to outplay the herbs themselves. This is an important point. Better too few flowering herbs than too many. I try to keep one border for herbs whose flowers are inconspicuous, letting the bed make its effect in subtleties and distinctions; the general "tussiemussie" beyond I open to both those with inconspicuous and more conspicuous blooms. None of the herbs I have listed will exactly overwhelm any border, but even then the distribution of flower color is something to plan with care, a garden problem to which there are as many pleasant answers as there are gardeners. In planning the garden itself, I think it best to avoid awhile the making of just one more formal border of perennials. Herbs do not really lend themselves particularly well to backgrounds and masses; their variations of height invite more imagination and subtlety. Taller ones are often very lovely when treated as isolated pillars skillfully placed and closed in upon by shorter herbs of suitable heights, and once a gardener has come to know herbs well, there is opened a whole new world of garden making in which to note, enjoy, and arrange the beautiful and living harmonies of green. If the gardener will remember that herbs are living things to be used in living ways, the garden will come to living beauty by its own natural paths.

LAVENDER

The matter of winter protection needs no special counsel. Many herbs are as hardy as plants of the north temperate zone can ever be, and those which need special winter protection have already been noted in the lists. The others the gardener can cover along with the rest of the garden in any favorite way he has found suited to his climate and latitude.

In gathering, preparing, and drying herbs, it is customary to cut the leaf stalks just before the plant flowers, the gathering to be made in the morning and on a warm sunshiny day and after the dew has left the leaves. All imperfect and withered leaves having been discarded, the herbs should be taken in loose, open bunches to some warm sunny room or attic and hung in the morning sun for half an hour, and then removed from the direct light and left to dry and crisp. When they have reached this state, the leaves should be stripped from the stalk, crumpled to the consistency the household prefers, and put away in sealed glass or china jars. Leaves for infusions or tisanes had best be left whole, and some prefer to leave them on the stalk and to keep a number of these bunches in a large, well-closed paper bag. Aromatic seeds are best dried by being shaken loosely upon a clean cloth laid in a wire box or colander standing in a warm place. In addition to tisanes and infusions and kitchen flavorings, all kinds of herbal patchoulis and potpourris can be made of the dried leaves and fruits. The skilled and imaginative have a field of their own in the invention of new and memorable cordials, the materials of the art being in their hands.

Not difficult to plan, not at all difficult to maintain, a garden of herbs gives more months of garden pleasure and more kinds of pleasure than any other. Its interest is independent of flowers, its fragrances are given from the first leaf to the last, its uses make it a part of the amenities of the whole year, and its history and traditions touch all nations and all times.

1. FRENCH NAMES OF THE HERBS CARRIED IN FRENCH CATALOGUES:

Agrimony, *Aigremoine*; Althea, *Guimauve*; Carduus Benedictus, *Chardon Bénit*; Fumitory, *Fumeterre*; Lovage, *Ache de Montagne*; Spike Vervain, *Verveine Officinale*; Woad or Isatis, *Pastel*.

2. TEN VERY HARDY HERB PERENNIALS:

Applemint (plain form), Lovage, Costmary,

Hyssop, Balm, Angelica, Comfrey, Wormwood (*A. Absinthium*), "Valerian" (*C. Ruber*), Chives.

3. HERBS WITH SIGNIFICANT FLOWERS:

Borage, "Valerian" (*C. Ruber*), Cerinthe, Althea, Clary, Goat's Rue, Pulmonaria, Pot Marjoram, Woad, Pot Marigold, Lavender.

4. TALLER HERBS:

Angelica, Lovage, Bayberry, Perennial Fennel, Carduus, Bee-Balm.

5. HERBS SUITABLE FOR EDGINGS:

Camomile, Burnet, Parsley, Dwarf Basil, Dwarf Lavender (*L. Nana Compacta*).

6. HERBS WHICH WILL STAND A DEAL OF SHADE:

Balm, any of the Mints, Sweet Woodruff, "Sweet Cicely" (European and native forms), Comfrey, Angelica, both Pennyroyals, Pulmonaria, Woundwort.

7. HERBS RECOMMENDED FOR HOUSE PLANTS:

Purple Basil, and Summer Savory (half a dozen seedling plants each to a flower pot eight inches in diameter): Rosemary, Lavender (*Lavandula Dentata*), Variegated Applemint, all three good as larger plants, especially Rosemary: Seedlings or small cuttings of Rue, Germander, Caraway-Thyme, Wild Thyme, Santolina, Pot Marjoram, Bergamot Mint, Balm, and English Pennyroyal, all excellent for small pots: the Bergamot and the Balm tending to assume a rather sprawly habit, the E. Pennyroyal being a true ground-runner. Those interested should try their individual luck with any herb which takes their fancy.

8. HERBS TRADITIONALLY ASSOCIATED WITH CULINARY USES:

The Savories, Garden Thyme, Sage, Basil, S. Marjoram, Tarragon.

9. MEDICINAL HERBS MOST IN HOUSEHOLD USE:

Wormwood (*A. Absinthium*), English and American Pennyroyal, Peppermint, Horehound, Catnip, Balm.

10. HERBS FOR TISANES:

Camomile Flowers, Spearmint, Peppermint, Monk's Herb, Sweet Woodruff.

11. GREAT MAGICAL HERBS:
Rue, Spike Vervain, Dill.

12. FLAVORING HERBS FOR GREEN SALADS:
Burnet, Chives, S. Marjoram, the Basils, Chervil, Dill (umbel and leaves); others may be found by the adventurous.

13. DRIED HERBS FOR FRAGRANCE:
Lavender leaves and Lavender seed, Rosemary leaves, Sweet Marjoram, Costmary, Bergamot Mint and Purple Basil leaves, Sweet Woodruff; Rose leaves may be added for color.

14. BIBLICAL HERBS DISCUSSED IN THIS BOOK:
Mandrake (Gen. 30, 14), Coriander (Ex. 16, 31), Wormwood (Rev. 8, 11), Mint (Luke 11, 42), Cumin (Isaiah 28, 25 & 27), "Anise"—the actual plant in question seems to have been Dill—(Mat. 23, 23), Hyssop (*Origanum Maru*) (John 19, 29), Saffron (Song of Songs 4, 14), Rue (Luke 11, 42).

EPILOGUE IN SPRING

CHAPTER V

Epilogue in Spring

THE EARTH EMERGES from the snow, lifting to
the reassurance of the longer day her fields that
have been as iron northward to the pole, a new
green lies in the dappled warmth upon the hill,
and the winter-barren trees are great with spring.
All day long, blown by a new and warmer wind,
loose ice and sailing floes from the ice remaining
on the lake have come tinkling like hollow glass
into the shallows of the coves, there to drift glint-
ing out of the light into the shadowy green of pines
once more reflected on quiet water, there to strand
and disappear. The waters under the earth and the
waters upon it are everywhere unsealing, flowing
from the new green of moss down the slope of
ledges in the sun and gathering in clearest pools
where the snow has melted in the woods. Crows

pass between the spring sky and the dead grass
touched with green, a new odor of water and
open earth is in the wind, a door of the house stands
open, and from a chimney-top a wreath of smoke
falls off and mingles with the sky.

In the garden of the herbs, where the drifts
stood so high, blown up the fenceless slope and
against the house from the northeast, the brighter
sun stands warm. Beneath their autumn covering
of leaves and hemlock boughs remaining green,
the mother roots stir in the earth, coming to life
in that darkness where, as George Herbert said,
they "keep house alone." Intricacy of leaf unborn,
color drawn upwards out of the earth, fragrance
and potency and beauty are here in secret being,
soon to be manifest to the several senses, and at
their roots a gift of the gardener's peace which
none shall have who have not a deep peace with
the earth, though the road to her seem but a path.
For beside that path lie the seasons and the ritual
of the year, the vast adventures and journeyings of
the sun, the towering of a wave to its breaking, the
faithful wheeling of the moon, the sound of rain
when there are no more leaves, and the furrow
lengthening under the tug of hoofs on a morning
in spring. Sustained and molded of its immeas-

urable forces, it is by this mystery we exist, and by its poetic power in our lives that we attain the stature of human beings, having the sun to our right hand and the earth and the seas beneath us; without it becoming like the ghosts in Homer, houseless, and thin and dead, and crowding and whispering angrily for blood.

The quiet of winter is wearing through upon the land. Human voices which seemed lost in the vast of snow have again the open earth beneath them, and over the unfrozen soil, across field and pasture and darker wood comes the bold and distant cry of chanticleer. What a fine sound it is, that triple and unearthly cry, heard here in the garden through the pale quiet of the northern spring. All the animal defiance of circumstance and fate, all the acceptance and challenge of the animal blood come with it into our human world seeking an echo there, before melting away into the light. Pressing on with the sun the furrow shall follow north the sun retreating, and the earth shall be sown again and shall part, giving life to the seed and to the herbs of man's remembrance, the ancient leaves dear at once to ploughman and woman of the distaff, to priest and golden-circleted king.

Index

HERBS AND THE EARTH

has been set on the Linotype at
The Shagbark Press of South Portland, Maine.
The type is Caslon Old Face. In terms of design, Caslon is really an
extension, perhaps a refinement, of its Dutch predecessors. It is most
successful in its middle sizes where its eccentricities of weight and
slope are not blatantly obvious. The roman is solid and sturdy but
light, a face that only looks proper when printed letterpress with real
impression. Despite its deficiencies, it remains a beloved face for many
English writers. G. B. Shaw and T. E. Lawrence both insisted that
all their books be printed in Caslon, and Shaw, with typical, ornery
cussedness, would sue the perpetrators of pirate editions not on
the basis of libel but because the type was not set in Caslon.

This offset edition has been printed and bound at the
Maple-Vail Book Manufacturing Group,
Binghamton, New York.